# RUFF'S WAR

## A Navy Nurse
## on the Frontline in Iraq

Cdr. Cheryl Lynn Ruff
U.S. Navy Nurse Corps (Ret.)

with

Cdr. K. Sue Roper
U.S. Navy Nurse Corps (Ret.)

Naval Institute Press
Annapolis, Maryland

Naval Institute Press
291 Wood Road
Annapolis, MD 21402

All photos are from the author's personal collection.

Library of Congress Cataloging-in-Publication Data

Ruff, Cheryl Lynn, 1958–
    Ruff's war : a Navy nurse on the frontline in Iraq / Cheryl Lynn Ruff ; with K. Sue
Roper.
        p. cm.
    ISBN 1-59114-739-5 (alk. paper)
    1. Iraq War, 2003—Personal narratives, American.   2. Iraq War, 2003—Medical
care—United States.   3. Ruff, Cheryl Lynn, 1958–   4. Nurses—United States—
Biography.   5. Nurses—Iraq—Biography.   I. Roper, K. Sue, 1952–   II. Title.
    DS79.76R84 2005
    956.7044'37—dc22

Printed in the United States of America on acid-free paper ♾

12 11 10 09 08 07 06 05     9 8 7 6 5 4 3 2
First printing

*To my sister, Jeryl Dean Kellett,*
*for her steadfast love and support throughout my career.*

*In memory of my cousin Kathy Lynn McKently,*
*who fought the most heroic battle.*

# Contents

| | | |
|---|---|---|
| *Acknowledgments* | | ix |
| *Abbreviations and Acronyms* | | xi |
| *Prologue: 3 April 2003* | | 1 |
| 1 | Early Inspirations | 3 |
| 2 | It's Not Just a Job, It's an Adventure | 13 |
| 3 | Being All That I Could Be | 26 |
| 4 | Anchors Aweigh | 41 |
| 5 | Deployment | 48 |
| 6 | Our New Home | 62 |
| 7 | Gearing Up for War | 70 |
| 8 | A Battle with Mother Nature | 77 |
| 9 | Settling Back In | 83 |
| 10 | Growing Weary | 90 |
| 11 | Heightened Alert and Final Preparations | 95 |
| 12 | War Is Declared | 104 |
| 13 | Moving North into Iraq | 112 |
| 14 | Camp Anderson: The Other Side of Hell | 122 |

15   Saving Lives                                    126

16   Caring for Jeff                                 135

17   We Are "Devil Docs"                             140

18   Surviving in the Wake of Death                  143

19   Camp Chesty                                     150

20   "Nesting" in Camp Chesty                        162

21   Stuck in Iraq                                   173

22   Back to the Beginning                           184

23   Welcome to the "Holiday Inn"                    188

24   There's No Place Like Home                      198

     *Epilogue*                                      205

     *Support Our Troops*                            207

     *About the Authors*                             209

# Acknowledgments

*Ruff's War: A Navy Nurse on the Frontline in Iraq* would not have been successful without the hard work and support of many individuals.

Special thanks to the writer K. Sue Roper, whose persistence and dedication made this book a reality.

To those who relentlessly insisted that my story be told: Phyllis Shelton, Betsy Nolan, Sandra Lindelof, Sandra "Sam" Yerkes, Nancy Lundquist, Peggy Dolan, Melinda Tankersley, Jan Reiff, James L. Roper III, Chic Lisitano, and Shirley Cornell.

To my family, friends, and all the employees and their families from Blue Ball National Bank, Blue Ball, Pennsylvania. Your encouragement, love, and support provided the strength I needed in the darkest hours.

# Abbreviations and Acronyms

| | |
|---|---|
| Alice | All-purpose lightweight individual carrying equipment |
| Ambu bag | Airway mask breathing unit; self-inflating bag that helps a patient breathe during resuscitation |
| AMMAL | Authorized minimum medical allowance list; medical and surgical equipment, supplies, and medications required by medical personnel to render care during conflicts and other contingencies |
| CAT scan | Computed axial tomography scan; an advanced non-invasive imaging technique that creates a full three-dimensional computer model of internal bones, organs, and body tissues and has the ability to examine one narrow slice at a time to pinpoint specific areas; more advanced and revealing than conventional X-ray imaging, which reveals only the outline of bones and organs |
| CPR | Cardiopulmonary resuscitation |
| CRNA | Certified registered nurse anesthetist |
| CVN | Multipurpose aircraft carrier (nuclear propulsion) |
| DDG | Guided missile destroyer |
| EMF | Expeditionary medical facility; facility with more staff and equipment than the field surgical companies |
| EPW | Enemy prisoner of war |
| EST | Eastern Standard Time |
| FITREP | Fitness report; a performance evaluation/appraisal for navy officers |

FRSS            Forward resuscitative support system

FSSG            Force service support group

ICU             Intensive care unit

ISO             International Organization for Standardization

LHA             Amphibious ship, multipurpose

LHD             Amphibious ship, general purpose

MEF             Marine Expeditionary Force

MOPP            Mission-oriented protective posture; clothing and special gear consisting of protective hood, battle-dress overgarment, overboots, butyl rubber gloves, gas mask, and gas mask filter

MRE             Meal ready to eat

MRI             Magnetic resonance imaging; a technique used primarily in medical settings to produce high-quality images of the inside of the human body; based on the principles of nuclear magnetic resonance (NMR), a spectroscopic technique used by scientists to obtain microscopic chemical and physical information about molecules

NMC             Naval Medical Center; formerly designated as Naval Hospital

NNMC            National Naval Medical Center (Bethesda, Maryland)

NSHS            Naval School of Health Sciences

OIS             Officer Indoctrination School

PACU            Post-anesthetic care unit

Stix            Transport grouping of twenty to twenty-four individuals

STP             Shock trauma platoon

T-AH            Hospital ship

# PROLOGUE

## 3 April 2003

We had no sooner set up the tents of our field hospital in Iraq than the helicopters began arriving with the dead and the wounded. We, the Bravo Surgical Company, were ready to go—prepared to triage, to perform surgery, to render all the medical and surgical care we could to those who were brought to us.

The first to be removed from a helicopter was a young American marine. He was carried off in a tarp, not in a body bag. One guy was holding one side of the tarp, and another was holding the other side as they carried him toward a large box that served as a morgue. I could see the top of this young marine's head. It was sticking out beyond the length of the tarp, and I could see his light brownish-blond hair. He could not have been any more than nineteen years old. I could also see his feet sticking out from the other end of the tarp. He was dead, and one of his boots had been removed in order to collect the dog tag that had been affixed to his left boot.

As he was carried past me, it hit me. This was war. People were shooting at us, trying to kill us. This was medical triage like I had never seen it before. Our young Americans were being shot and killed, and I

1

knew that I was in a situation where I was just as much a target of the enemy as were the combat marines. Still, what frightened me more than my own mortality was the question of my ability, and I could not help but think, "Will I be able to handle, within my own mind, body, soul, and spirit, the horrendous devastation of humanity that I will not only be a witness to but also a primary player in offering healing and comfort? God give me the strength to make the right decisions for my patients. These guys need us now."

# 1

# EARLY INSPIRATIONS

While I was growing up in Fleetwood, Pennsylvania, during the 1960s and 1970s, war was the last thing on my mind. I was too busy being a child, trying to discover who I was, and wondering where my life was going to ponder such major mind-boggling, incomprehensible issues as war and death. I never thought I would one day be in the middle of a war, directly witnessing its horrors and doing everything in my power to save the lives of the men, women, and children who would be brutally wounded as a result of fighting in a place halfway around the world. Yet, in many ways, my relationships with family and friends, my cherished memories, and the lessons I learned as I grew and matured to young adulthood would prepare me for and provide me with comfort and support throughout my journey of sacrifice and survival in the bloody, turbulent, and war-torn sands of Iraq.

I was born on 21 January 1958 in Reading, Pennsylvania, just twelve miles from Fleetwood. Fleetwood was no different from most other small rural hometowns. Everyone knew one another and often would be related to each other, because many would marry the girl or boy next door, have children who grew to adults, who would also marry the girl or boy next door, and they, too, would have children. Several generations of one family resided in Fleetwood and would continue to remain living there throughout their lives. Both my mother's and my father's parents lived there, as did several of my parents' siblings, and I was fortunate to be surrounded by grandparents, uncles, aunts, and cousins throughout the growing-up days of my first seventeen years.

Both my maternal grandparents (the McKentlys) and my paternal grandparents (the Ruffs) lived less than two miles from our home, and although they were polar opposites in the ways they showed their love and affection, I did feel their love and support of me as a child and for many years beyond.

My father's side of the family was open, warm, and demonstrative. Hugs, generous snacks, gifts, and various other forms of love and affection were readily offered and exchanged. My sister and I, along with several of my cousins, would spend many hours at Grandma and Grandpa Ruff's home, visiting, playing, and simply basking in the love and adoration we felt from them.

Coming from a strict German Mennonite line of descent, my grandparents on my mother's side were closed, rigid, and highly disciplined, and they did not readily show their feelings or affections. Generally noncommunicative, neither my Grandmother McKently nor, especially, my grandfather talked very much, and we found it almost impossible to determine what they were thinking or feeling most of the time. My most vivid memory and image of Grandfather McKently, and one I would often think of as the years of my navy career passed by, is a simple one, and recalling it would always bring a smile to my face. One day while he sat, seemingly focused and concentrating only on rubbing off the salt from a hard Pennsylvania Dutch pretzel using his massive sausage-like fingers, he turned to me and said, "So will you be making the navy a career?" I had only been in the navy a few months and had no real answer to his question. Because he was a man of few words, I was so surprised by his interest in me and my future that I do not really know what I said to him. Had I known then what I know now, and had I not been so startled by this lengthy verbalization from such a quiet, closed man, I would have responded, "Yes, I think I will make it a career, and I believe it will be a good one."

My mother, Esther, was a self-employed hairdresser. Her beauty shop was connected to our house, and her regular weekly customers watched my sister and me grow up as my mother diligently cut, permed, curled, and colored their hair, all the while listening to their stories and helping them solve problems. Her customers would arrive for their appointments at the same time and on the same day every week throughout the fifty-two weeks of the year, and they would leave Mom's shop with the same hairstyle week after week. Viewing these women through the eyes of a child, I thought they all seemed old. Still, they all left feeling good about themselves, and as I watched my mom work her magic, I began to learn some very valuable lessons.

As Mom would work in her shop, or when she would go to the hospital and even periodically to the funeral home to coif the hair of one of her regular customers, she instilled within me the values of hard work, customer service, honesty, integrity, the importance of caring for others, and even the independent strength and willpower that were gender neutral. Mom may have been a female, but she was also strong willed and very determined to do anything and everything for the good of her family. Whereas many in her generation would be passive, dependent victims and would choose to embrace the housewife role that was prevalent throughout the sixties and seventies, my mom was anything but passive and dependent. Mom was our family's breadwinner, the disciplinarian, the cook, and even "the dad." Well ahead of her time, she possessed tremendous strength and a sense of "woman power" that would grow to be popular and readily accepted later in the eighties and nineties. As I watched her work day after day, I developed and embraced the notion that I could grow up to be an astronaut, a jet pilot, or just about anything else I desired. I was bound only by my own physical limitations, my desire, my drive, and my personal resolve.

My dad, Lester, made storage containers on an assembly line in the town's local factory. Because my mom and dad divorced when I was two years old, I have no memory of him living with us, but, along with my sister, Jeryl, I would continue to see, visit, and share many adventures with him throughout my childhood, adolescence, and young adulthood.

Dad was a World War II navy veteran who had served as a gunner's mate on a tanker. He loved the navy and would often delight us in singing every verse of "Anchors Aweigh." It amazed us that he knew every word of every verse of that song, and Jeryl and I would always join him in singing the chorus. To this day, after having served twenty-five years in the navy, I can say that Dad has been the only person I have ever known who could sing every word of "Anchors Aweigh" by heart. His singing, his sea stories, and his love of the navy significantly influenced me to join the navy later in life and to make it my career. I will always remember him telling me that, unlike life in the U.S. Army or Marine Corps, life in the U.S. Navy would guarantee a roof over my head and never having to sleep on the ground outside in the open—a true guarantee for *his days* in the navy, perhaps. I would eventually discover life in the navy to be very different, especially once I entered the war-torn nation of Iraq, where there would be no real guarantees.

When I was seven years old, my mom remarried. Her new husband's name was Bud, and he was a salesman of beauty supplies. Mom and Bud met when he came to the shop marketing his wares. He would remain a permanent fixture in my home as my stepfather, supporting and reinforcing Mom's established rules by which my sister and I were being raised.

My "big sister" has been watching out for me, giving me advice, acting as my protector, and always being there for me, no matter what, throughout my forty-seven years of life and especially during my harrowing, dangerous, and unsettled days spent in Iraq. My mother had always dreamed of having twin daughters, and so she gave Jeryl and me same-sounding names, even though our birth dates are separated by fourteen months. Throughout our childhood years we forged a solid, indestructible, loving bond that honored and respected our individual and unique differences.

When Mom named us, she had no idea that Jeryl and I would be polar opposites in our interests, our activities, and even our appearance. We definitely were not the identical twins for which she was hoping. Where Jeryl sported long dark hair, had dark eyes, and was tall and of medium build, I was light haired, had hazel eyes, and was much shorter in stature. Jeryl hated to get her hands dirty or her hair messed. She often spent hours coloring her nails, coifing her hair, applying makeup, or just primping in front of the mirror. She was the little girl most mothers probably dreamed of and desired most. I, on the other hand, was the tomboy, caring little about what I looked like and always wanting to be outside playing, climbing trees, riding my bike, or being involved in whatever rough-and-tumble activity I could find. The dirtier I got, the happier I was.

I would never be able to understand why Jeryl or anyone else would want to spend a beautiful sunny day indoors when Mother Nature was providing me with bugs to dissect, trees to climb, and a beautiful big sky under which I could launch my homemade rockets during the day and peer up at the brilliant twinkling stars at night, imagining all that lay beyond. I would often spend hours in the yard with my telescope watching the stars and dreaming of becoming an astronaut.

As Jeryl and I grew older, our radical differences became even more apparent in our dreams and desires for the future. Jeryl had no desire to attend college. Wanting to enter the workforce quickly and begin making money, she took the "commercial" route of subjects and studies during high school, excelling in math, shorthand, and typing. Jeryl was a true businesswoman in the making and was born to be a banker. As little sisters did then and continue to do now, I was relentless in my attempts to disrupt her focus, serving as a constant pest and distraction as she devoted hour after hour to practicing and refining her shorthand skills and techniques. I just simply could not understand her desire to sit inside the house scribbling on a steno pad as she listened to 45-rpm talk records designed specifically for shorthand practice when it was so warm, sunny, and beautiful outdoors. The summer weather was perfect for playing, exploring, and simply having fun!

Winters in Fleetwood were bitterly cold. Outdoor play or almost any other outside activity was highly undesirable, unless one wanted to freeze or be subject to frostbite. As Jeryl continued with her shorthand practice, I would often be in the basement trying to figure out how to get my Bunsen burner to work or dissecting the goldfish I would get out of my mother's pond. Mom did not know I was the one responsible for the disappearing goldfish; she believed the cat next door was eating them.

In ninth grade I signed up for a class in taxidermy. My mother once discovered me in the basement gutting and skinning a squirrel that had been given to me by a hunter. She was so angry, her jugular veins protruded on the sides of her neck, her eyes bulged from their sockets, and she screamed, "Get that damn thing out of this house right now!" I was shocked by her reaction because I saw very little wrong with what I was doing and had planned to clean up the bloody mess I was making. I thought I was doing the smart thing by pursuing this activity indoors, especially because it was wintertime and so cold outside. Still, I learned a valuable lesson that day. I needed to be much more discreet and well away from my mother as I continued to practice my dissection technique in my exploration of the internal anatomy and physiology of fish and small mammals.

Mom was not an openly demonstrative woman, and at times it was difficult to know what she was thinking except when she was angry. Still, she was an eternal optimist, constantly reassuring us and telling us that whatever we were facing would be okay and that everything would work out. She was also determined that her two daughters would grow up learning to be independent and self-supporting.

Despite Mom's divorce from my father when I was a toddler, she continued to maintain a close, friendly relationship with my fraternal grandparents. They were very much a mainstay during my childhood and would continue sharing their sage advice, their love, and their support of me as I grew up and set my sail toward a career in the navy.

Many times Jeryl would accompany me as we trekked off to my father's parents' home. It was not easy prying her away from her "girlie" preoccupation with her hair, nails, and clothing, but when we did play together, we always had great fun and continued to recognize and appreciate one another for the individuals that we were.

When Jeryl was not around or was too preoccupied with her short-hand or self-beautification pursuits, I was fortunate enough to be able to play instead with the several cousins who resided in the neighborhood. We were all close to the same age, and I spent numerous hours with them, playing, attending school together, and having sleepovers at each other's homes. We developed such a close bond that we became more like brothers and sisters instead of simply cousins. Competitive in some activities, we also learned to share, cooperate, work together on common projects, and respect our individual differences. These lessons learned would be very valued and important to me as I got older and would serve me well as I found myself sharing a variety of play, work, and even living situations with various colleagues throughout my navy career.

Among all my cousins, Kathy was closest to me, and we shared many of the same interests. Being "best friends," we were inseparable, always sitting next to each other and always steadfastly insisting that we be put on the same team at family gatherings. We were very much the two tomboys of our group, active in numerous sports, and we simply relished all that made up our small world in Fleetwood. Despite the many years that would pass and the different roads we would choose to travel, Kathy and I would remain close and spiritually bonded to the bitter end.

As a family we took occasional vacations, and when we did they were usually educational in nature. We would venture to somewhere in western Pennsylvania to visit a museum or historical landmark. Wanting to be more physically active and to ski, ride surfboards, paddle a kayak, or canoe down the Colorado River and move well beyond the confines of my home state, I would often find myself bored and dreaming of what lay beyond. My sense of wonder and my lust to travel were quickly developing; I fervently wanted to get out of Pennsylvania, to see what the other side of the world was like.

My interest in anatomy, physiology, and the other sciences had continued all through high school. By the time I reached my senior year, I had become fascinated with the merging of science and technology evident in the country's evolving space program and closely followed all the space flights of the Mercury, Gemini, and Apollo programs. I was well versed in the specific scientific data and conditions of every mission, and in my heart I wanted more than anything else to be an astronaut. I knew that in order to qualify for and have any chance of becoming an astronaut, I would need college, instruction as a pilot, and even military training because all of the astronauts of that era were military pilots.

Both of my parents were very supportive of my dreams, but they were also staunch believers in the concept that if you really wanted something, you needed to get out, work for it, and pay your own way. I soon learned that my poor eyesight, which had plagued me since I was two years old, would disqualify me from becoming a pilot. Without pilot training—a requirement for all astronauts in those early days—I would have no chance of realizing my dream of becoming an astronaut. Somewhat disheartened, I still knew that I wanted to work in a science-related field, whatever that field might be. The thought of becoming a nurse never entered my mind, not even in my wildest dreams.

I visited Bryn Mawr University, located nine miles west of Philadelphia, to research their veterinarian assistant program. I applied and was thrilled when I received my notification of acceptance. Unfortunately, the numerous applications I sent out for scholarships, loans, and grants were denied. Not knowing of the navy's Reserve Officers' Training Corps program, I believed that my only option was to go to work, labor long and hard, and eventually earn the money to pay the tuition for higher education.

A few months shy of high school graduation, and after receiving my mother's permission and support, I decided to make a visit to the local navy recruiter. Why the navy? It was not about the uniforms, and it was not that the navy would provide me with anything different or special from what was being offered by the other military service branches. It was simply because my dad had been in the navy, and I remembered how highly he had regarded it.

Pre-enlistment testing revealed I was qualified academically for navy enlistment because I scored high in areas of mechanical engineering and all of the other science-related fields. My physical examination was unremarkable with the exception of my eyesight. The medical examiners reconfirmed my worst fear; my eyesight was too poor for me to ever qualify as a pilot. I would never forget them saying, "You can take off; you just can't land." Because there was no such thing as laser eye surgery in the early seventies, I had no choice but to resign myself completely to the realization that I would never be a military pilot, let alone an astronaut. Instead, I knew I needed to find a new field of interest and could only hope the navy had something to offer me that would develop into a personal passion.

The navy recruiter called to give me the good news of my military enlistment qualifications. I was "in," and he proceeded to provide me with a long list of job openings that were related to both mechanical engineering and science. The only opening that sounded even close to my second career choice was "medical."

As he explained the role of the navy hospital corpsman, I grew very excited not only with the concept of performing general medical and nursing duties but also at the prospect that I might be able to see surgical procedures being performed and even someday be able to assist with those procedures. I really had no idea what I was signing up for, but I did want to learn and work in an area that explored how things worked, what held them together, and how they were put back together again.

I also hoped that the navy would provide me with experiences, opportunities, and training that would serve as stepping-stones for a more specific and higher-level health-related technical profession. In addition, the navy offered the thrilling prospect of worldwide travel and the ability to move well beyond the small boundaries of Pennsylvania. I would be able to see firsthand what was out there on the other side of the world. I was easily sold on enlisting in the navy and signed on immediately.

Still having a few months of high school remaining before graduation, I continued working part-time at McDonald's and dreaming of the adventure that lay ahead. For an additional eight months following graduation, I remained in Fleetwood working full-time, watching my high school friends leave for colleges and universities, and eagerly awaiting the time when I would be able to start my new career. The wait seemed interminable, but in order to be assured that I could attend Hospital Corps School immediately following nine weeks of basic training, I would not be able to leave for boot camp until 14 February 1976, not even a month after turning eighteen years of age.

# 2

# IT'S NOT JUST A JOB, IT'S AN ADVENTURE

Shortly after my eighteenth birthday, I was sworn in as a seaman recruit (E-1) in the U.S. Navy. My mother and Bud were there to bid me farewell as I boarded the train in Mechanicsville, Pennsylvania, and headed to Orlando, Florida. I had no idea what to expect or what my future would hold other than nine weeks of boot camp followed by Hospital Corps School in Great Lakes, Illinois. I was scared, but I was also very excited to explore the unknown world I was entering. This was a new adventure, and I could only hope and pray it would prove to be an adventure of a lifetime, filled with fun, excitement, and memorable moments. It would prove to be all of those and then some.

The train ride to Orlando was fifteen hours long. Much of that time I spent studying the twelve critical points of standing a military guard post. We would be required to memorize these points and be ready to recite them on request throughout boot camp.

Exhausted from the train ride, excited, and still a little scared because I had never before ventured so far from home alone, I met up upon arriving at the Orlando train depot with several others who were also headed to the navy's East Coast U.S. Naval Recruit Training

Command. We gathered together and used the train station's direct phone line to call for transportation that would take us to boot camp.

An old gray government bus rumbled to a stop at the curbside where we had all gathered. As the bus doors opened, our first glimpse of the fierce and aloof driver increased my anxiety. She barely looked at us before harshly barking, "Get on the bus and keep your mouths shut!" We all scrambled to get on the bus and sat quietly on the ratty, uncomfortable seats. I did not realize at the time that the train depot and what little I could see from the bus window as we traveled to the command would be the last glimpse of the world outside the confines of a wired fence for nine long, grueling, yet also very enlightening weeks.

Besides being constantly screamed and barked at while at boot camp, we were taught about integrity, honesty, taking care of one another, and always looking out for our shipmates because each person's life was just as important as our own. Because my mom and my dad had provided me with a firm foundation and strong moral code specific to honesty, integrity, and respect for others, I found these lessons easy. I respected authority, did what I was told, and willingly worked as a team member. We spent numerous hours and days marching on the grinder (a large outdoor concrete slab); carefully folding and storing our clothes; and starching, pressing, and scrupulously adorning our uniforms so that we were meticulously groomed in accordance with the very rigid and strict regulations of the U.S. Navy.

A total of seventy-five women made up our company, and our berthing barracks featured little more than bunk-bed racks and lockers. We would join other recruit companies, many of them consisting of our male counterparts, in the chow hall, where everyone was ordered to keep both hands and forearms on top of the table at all times to prevent any under-the-table clandestine physical contact with one another. Given fifteen minutes to eat, we totally discarded our table manners as we reached over each other, grabbing for whatever table condiments were available and quickly shoveling food into our mouths. Our barbaric table manners and customs were not the most positive of lessons learned, and it would take me weeks following my boot camp experience to break these primitive, unrefined, and highly unattractive habits.

One of the most valuable lessons I learned during recruit training, and one that I carried with me throughout my career, was the importance of attention to detail. This lesson was drilled into us constantly, reinforced over and over during numerous personnel, barracks, and locker inspections. If our underwear was found to be one-sixth of an inch off from being folded in accordance with strict and detailed directives, the entire contents of our locker would be thrown out, requiring hours to meticulously refold, align, and put back each item in accordance with the locker storage directives. If the mattress was found to be out of exact alignment with the frame of your rack during a barracks inspection or if the bed was improperly made, the inspectors would tear sheets and mattresses off the bed frames, and you would return to a barracks that was in shambles, a chaotic mess with mattresses, sheets, and pillows strewn everywhere.

Although I would not realize it at the time, these lessons in detail and the importance of attending to every one of them would serve me well. Having fully incorporated this attentiveness skill and trait into my personality, I would ultimately spread my keen sense and responsibility to attend to various details to all aspects of my personal and professional life. That which I had learned at the beginning of my career would be applied throughout my career and would save me at its end.

During our weeks at the U.S. Naval Recruit Training Command, Orlando, we had no access to radios, television, newspapers, or anything else that would provide us with news of the outside world. We were totally isolated in our own little world; I would not even learn the full extent of the kidnapping of Patty Hearst until after boot camp graduation.

When I reported to boot camp, the kidnapping of Patty Hearst was national news and was being followed by most American households and many others throughout the world. The last report I had heard prior to starting boot camp was that Patty Hearst had been kidnapped. After graduating, and while driving back with my mother to

Pennsylvania, I asked, "What happened to Patty Hearst?" She looked at me with an incredulous expression and said, "You don't know?" I very much disliked being out of touch with what was happening in the world, yet I would later learn that the restrictive nature of boot camp would be tame in comparison to that which I would encounter in my future.

The fourth week of boot camp was known as "hell week," where each of us was assigned to work in various areas and operational positions throughout the base that supported the care and feeding of all recruits stationed there. My week was spent steaming and cleaning dishes in the scullery twelve to fourteen hours each day. It was physically brutal, hot, and exhausting work, and the harsh conditions in which we worked would even contribute to one of my shipmates' experiencing a seizure. Still, I was fortunate, and after working hard during hell week and throughout the nine weeks I was stationed at the U.S. Navy Recruit Training Command, I graduated from boot camp unscathed. I had survived the first hurdle of my navy career feeling physically stronger, more confident, and proud. With this new sense of pride in being a U.S. Navy sailor, I traveled on to Hospital Corps School at Great Lakes, Illinois.

I liked Hospital Corps School even though it was bloody cold in Illinois. It was only May, and I could not imagine what the weather must have been like during the winter months. Still, I enjoyed the classes, and during the fourteen weeks of training I learned a great deal about human anatomy and physiology and how to provide patient care. I believed I had made a good decision by going into a medical-related field, but I also had some reservations.

The science and nursing courses were interesting and challenging, and practicing lab skills as a group was fun. Still, my first experience with providing patient care was awkward, messy, and unimpressive. I had tried to do all I could for this patient, a severely debilitated elderly woman who, having been incontinent during the night, had dried feces caked on her entire backside. Handling this situation would be my first real patient bed-bath opportunity, and I was at a loss. Being out of my element, I remember thinking, "What have I gotten myself into, and how do I get myself out of this?" I was not sure I had selected the right profession for myself, and I knew I would need much more guidance and assistance from individuals other than those who had thus far served as my mentors.

Throughout boot camp and Hospital Corps School, most of my authority figures were senior enlisted personnel, and I looked on them as if they were gods. The contact I had with commissioned officers, including those in the Navy Nurse Corps, was minimal. It would not be until I arrived at the Naval Hospital, Long Beach, California, that I would find myself being significantly influenced by navy nurses.

Upon graduating from Hospital Corps School, I was thrilled to have received orders to California. In my mind, California represented beaches, and I wanted the opportunity to spend time on those beaches swimming and learning how to surf. A world filled with sand, sun, warm temperatures, and fun was waiting for me, and I could not wait to go.

In August 1976 I arrived at the Naval Hospital in Long Beach and was assigned to an all-female surgical ward. Many of the staff on the ward consisted of civilian care providers; I was one of only two active-duty corpsmen assigned there. My charge nurse—the overall manager of this ward—was a male navy nurse who was a lieutenant at the time, but, as was the custom in the navy in the seventies, we called him "mister" instead of using his rank. Lt. Irv Ames used to tease me and challenge me to become more proficient in my nursing skills. When another enlisted female corpsman reported to the ward, "Mr. Ames" turned to me and jokingly said, "Teach her everything you know. That should take about two minutes." He was a good guy and fun to work with, and he provided me with many valuable experiences and opportunities.

That unit's nursing staff, civilian nurses and the few navy nurses with whom I would have contact while working the three different shifts, was wonderful, and I viewed these folks as my family. I lived in the barracks adjacent to the hospital, and, not owning a car at that time, I had no opportunity to venture to the beach. So, I would often go back to the ward just to see this new family of mine and to visit them even when I was off duty. If they were busy and needed an extra hand, I was always willing to pitch in and do whatever I could to help lessen their workload.

I worked various eight-hour shifts, frequently alongside a navy nurse because during the night shift the unit was staffed with only one nurse and one corpsman. Some of the navy nurses intimidated me more than others simply because of their rigidly starched, serious, and professional dress and persona. One such nurse was Ens. Brigit Balog.

Ensign Balog was a no-nonsense, conscientious nurse who took nothing for granted. She expected her staff to be on their toes at all times, efficiently and effectively attending to every detail of patient care. She not only wanted patient-care procedures performed correctly but also insisted that we understand why the procedures were being performed. Because she was serious and demanding, working for Ensign Balog was a challenge, and although I was scared of her, I also greatly admired her proficiency and dedication toward providing exceptional patient care.

Fascinated and impressed by the nurses' ability to give the change-of-shift report, I just could not imagine how they were able to remember and report to the oncoming shift all the specific details regarding the medical and nursing care of each patient. We had twenty to thirty patients on the ward at any given time and what seemed like more than a hundred details that needed to be passed along to ensure continuity of care. "Passing report," which is what the change-of-shift report was known as, was amazing to me, and I also saw it as a challenge that I wanted to take on.

One night, during the 11 PM to 7 AM shift, I mustered my courage and asked Ensign Balog whether I might have an opportunity to give the passing report. She asked me, "Do you think you could?" I looked at her and replied, "I don't know, but I'd like to give it a try." Whether it was the determination she saw in my eyes or my eagerness to grow and move beyond my status as a general-duty corpsman, she took me under her wing, showing me what she did and how she was able to acquire the pertinent and critical information that would ensure a comprehensive and informative patient-care change-of-shift report.

The morning I was to give the report, I was so nervous I was physically shaking, for I was the first corpsman assigned to this particular nursing unit who would attempt to successfully master what I saw as an awesome feat. I desperately wanted to do it right. Ensign Balog was there in the crowded nurses' station supporting me and giving me the boost of confidence I needed. She seemed to believe in me and in my abilities more than I did, and her presence, combined with the confidence I saw in her eyes, was just what I needed most. My passing report that day was a huge success. It was a wonderful and heady experience for me, and I thought no position could get any better. It was my day, my brief moment to shine, and I was in my glory. That day the spark of someday becoming a registered nurse was ignited in my mind.

The intensive care unit (ICU) was just outside the ward on which I was assigned, and every day as I reported for duty, I would pass by it and look through its door. I was intrigued by what I saw. The patients in the ICU were critically ill, and I could see that those who were providing care within the unit were intelligent and highly skilled. They were very impressive to me. The ICU and those who worked within it piqued my interest and helped further fan the flame of my desire for the profession of nursing.

My experience at Naval Hospital, Long Beach, was very positive even though it was also the place I would witness my first death. The patient was an elderly woman who had a do-not-resuscitate (DNR) order. She was slowly dying and close to death, but never having seen someone die, I did not understand what was truly happening. After observing her slow, labored, and irregular breathing pattern, I quickly found one of the nurses and hysterically asked, "What are we going to do?" The nurse signaled me to be calm, and we went back into the patient's room, adjusted her sheets and covers to make her as comfortable as possible, and remained with her as she died. It was an eerie experience, but I learned the importance of allowing someone to die calmly, peacefully, as comfortably as possible, and with dignity.

For several days after this event, the nurses were very attentive to me and to my emotional needs related to witnessing this death. They wanted to be sure I was doing okay, and they supported me as I came to grips with the finality of death within my eighteen-year-old adolescent mind and heart. The care and compassion shown to me by those nurses during the year I spent on the ward at Long Beach would ultimately play a decisive role in my future decision to go into the nursing profession.

While stationed at Long Beach I had saved my money and eventually was able to purchase my first car. I was also able to purchase a surfboard, and instead of spending all my off-duty time on the ward or in the barracks, I was soon out on the beach learning to surf and having a wonderful time. I worked hard, played hard, and slept little. To this day, I do not really know how I did it all.

After spending several months serving as a general-duty corpsman on the ward, I was encouraged to apply to an advanced Hospital Corps "C" School program. "C" is the designation the navy medical department gives to specialized advanced training programs that go beyond the basic general nursing care instruction received at Hospital Corps School. Those who graduate from one of these programs receive the title of technician, as compared to the title general-duty corpsman, which is equivalent to being a nursing aide. Working as a technician, I would have more stabilized working hours instead of the constantly rotating shift work inherent in working as a ward corpsman. Regular work hours were especially important because they would give me the opportunity to take college courses on my off-duty time. The nurses had allowed me to administer medications on the ward, but only after I was able to tell them all about the desired effects of the drug, its side effects, and why the patient was receiving the drug. As a result, I became very interested in pharmacodynamics and pharmacokinetics and wanted to learn more.

I applied and was accepted to the Pharmacy Technician "C" School at the Naval School of Health Sciences in San Diego. My class comprised only sixteen students, and I found the course material difficult and very challenging. I enjoyed the courses, and the more I got into the subject matter, the more I liked it. It was science, general chemistry, and pharmaceutical compounding, and I was fascinated by how the drugs and medications interacted with the body's system. Despite experiencing a freak racquetball accident that resulted in several days of hospitalization with both of my eyes patched, I was allowed to continue in my class, and kept up by listening to audiotape lectures. After being discharged from the hospital, I returned to school and was able to pass the quizzes and tests successfully, ultimately graduating second in my class.

Although I really wanted to stay in California, close to the beach where I could continue to surf, my next set of military orders—and the first as a pharmacy technician—were to Naval Hospital, Orlando, Florida. I reported to the hospital's pharmacy in March 1978, and I would remain there for a little less than a year.

I enjoyed the central Florida area with its sweet smell of orange blossoms and the slow-moving, swaggering families of peacocks that often blocked our drive to work. I especially loved my job. Responsible for the compounding section of the pharmacy, I made numerous drugs and intricate medicinal compounds for dermatology; ear, nose, and throat; and various other specialized units and areas throughout the hospital. Although I was just a few months beyond my twentieth birthday, my responsibilities included weighing out precise quantities of cocaine and accounting for every milligram of it. I loved making the various emulsions and compounds; it was like being Betty Crocker every day, and it was great!

I developed a strong sense of responsibility and continued learning more and more about the various pharmaceutical agents, ingredients, and products. I also became acutely aware of how easy it was for others to abuse these drugs and how they could mess up a person's mind to the point where some individuals would go to almost any length to acquire controlled substances and get their "fix." That was an important lesson for me, and to this day the medications and narcotics I use in my anesthesia practice are rigidly controlled and never left lying around in a drawer or even placed on a table outside of my direct eyesight.

My thirst for knowledge and desire for continuing education led me to enroll in a few general college courses at Valencia Community College in Orlando. I began my pursuit for higher education by enrolling in English and math classes two nights a week. Although these classes were not always exciting or stimulating, I knew they were valuable stepping stones that would provide me an opportunity to grow and move into a professional field of my own choosing. Because the navy was helping to subsidize the tuition for these courses, I had very little to lose and a lot to gain.

During my first few months in Orlando, I lived in the barracks but soon moved into a small one-bedroom first-floor apartment with another female corpsman who hailed from Fort Lauderdale. That Fourth of July weekend, my roommate had planned to go home but was unable to do so because of a schedule change. She was very disappointed, but to this day I believe God was looking out for us and prevented her from leaving me alone in the apartment that night.

Sometime in the middle of the night, I heard my roommate get up to go into the bathroom, and when she came back toward the bedroom, I heard her say in a very strained, scared, and shrill voice, "Cheryl!" I immediately began screaming, jumped out of bed, and grabbed a marble knickknack from the table situated between our two beds. I could see the silhouette of a man reflected on the wall as he stood in our apartment's living room. I then heard the door slam. Because it was so dark, I was not sure whether the man had fled or was still inside our apartment. Shuffling into our small kitchenette, my roommate immediately behind me, I instinctively grabbed a butcher knife, and we began turning on all the lights. Fortunately, the man had fled, and we found that only the two of us remained in the apartment. This experience was so frightening that it did not seem real, but real it was, as the popped-open screen of the low window adjacent to the door would testify.

That experience was a defining moment for me. I found that although I had always slept soundly throughout the night in total blackness for twenty years, from then on I always needed a light source and some ability to see what was happening around me. If disaster was to strike, and I was put in harm's way, I wanted to be a witness to it and have a fighting chance and some sense of control, rather than to be nothing more than a simple, passive victim. This innate desire would grow to be instinctual in me.

In January 1979, I headed back to San Diego. I had agreed to swap positions with one of the other pharmacy technicians, who desperately wanted to return to the East Coast. My dad flew down to Orlando from Pennsylvania, and together we drove cross-country. We had a fantastic time, celebrating my twenty-first birthday together, listening to the play-by-play action of the Super Bowl on the car radio, and just being together riding in the car. It would also be the last time I would have the opportunity to spend any quality time with him.

My San Diego orders were to the navy's branch clinic in Coronado, where a total of only four pharmacy technicians were assigned to cover the North Island and the Coronado area. Our beneficiaries were primarily retired senior officers, and we were extremely busy filling multiple prescriptions, providing detailed medication administration instructions, and ensuring the efficacy and proficiency of our pharmaceutical-dispensing practice. In addition to our normal workday schedule, we had duty five times a week, during which time our primary role was one of general-duty corpsman. This duty entailed riding in ambulances and responding to emergency calls, performing cardiopulmonary resuscitation (CPR) and basic life support, suturing lacerations, and developing skills as emergency medicine personnel. I loved the excitement and the adrenaline surge that I experienced during these emergency ambulance runs and knew I wanted to grow and develop well beyond my current role as a pharmacy technician.

When not on duty, I spent my time surfing and running. I was also relentless in my pursuit of a college degree; I enrolled in several night courses at San Diego Community College throughout the remainder of my initial four-year enlistment obligation. I had spent almost five years as an enlisted member in the navy, and I wanted more than anything to become a commissioned officer. As a third-class petty officer and designated pharmacy technician, I greatly enjoyed working in the pharmacy. I knew I wanted to stay in a medical-related field, but I struggled with deciding what my future career choice should be. I saw becoming a pharmacist and becoming a registered nurse as two very viable and attractive future possibilities.

I sat down with a good friend, Cdr. Shirley (Richard) Cornell, a nurse with whom I had previously been stationed at Long Beach, and her husband, Capt. Gordon Cornell, U.S. Navy, and we talked about my interests and prospects for the future. Shirley had previously helped me acquire letters of recommendation and complete my application for pharmacy technician school early in my career. Since our days at Long Beach, we had continued to stay in contact through letters, phone calls, and visits, including one that involved attending Shirley's wedding to Gordon. I especially saw a lot of Shirley after she and Gordon each received orders to San Diego. I had grown to know both of them well. Highly successful individuals, they were my friends, and I trusted their guidance, for I knew they both cared about me very much and wanted to help me make choices that would be the right ones for me.

Gordon, a navy line officer in charge of the Rework Facility for F-4 Phantoms at North Island, Coronado, California, recommended that I look at the possibility of attending the U.S. Naval Academy. He assured me that if I decided to go to the academy, he would make it a reality for me. Being provided with four years of college plus room and board at no cost to me was a very tempting prospect, but, unfortunately, at that time the U.S. Naval Academy did not offer collegiate degrees in any medical-related field. I did think a lot about it, yet I soon realized a degree in engineering or some other field not even remotely related to medicine was not what I wanted to do.

Shirley was a tremendous mentor for me, guiding and supporting my decision-making process without overly influencing its outcome. The only thing she was adamant about was that I would not settle for an associate degree no matter what field I chose to enter. She believed in me and in my abilities to obtain a bachelor's degree and eventually a master's. I loved pharmacy, but I knew that as a pharmacist my interaction with patients would be limited and that I would miss that very personal aspect of health care. I had loved the days I spent on the ward in Long Beach and the emergency medicine experience I had while in Coronado. Shirley helped me put it all in perspective one day when she said, "You know, Cheryl, you're going to do pharmacy every day as a nurse, but you're not going to do nursing as a pharmacist. You'll have very little interaction with the patients unless you are always right there at the window when the patients come to pick up their prescriptions."

Gordon then introduced me to Holly, the daughter of a navy helicopter pilot whom Gordon had known for many years. Holly was enrolled in nursing school at Fort Hays University in western Kansas. We met when she came to visit her family over the Christmas holidays. Although I wanted to stay in California very much, Holly's description of the nursing program structured in eight-week modules versus semesters greatly appealed to me. I applied to Fort Hays University and was thrilled when I found out they were willing to accept all of my previous course credits, plus enroll me at the sophomore level. My decision was made, and I had no regrets as I packed my old 1976 Mustang with my few personal belongings, attached my surfboard to its roof, and headed east to western Kansas, a place to which I had never been nor ever dreamed I would be.

# 3

# BEING ALL THAT I COULD BE

Academic courses at Fort Hays University began in September 1980. I was still on active-duty status but had purposefully saved my terminal leave days in order to ensure that I would be free to start classes on schedule. That year, my summer vacation was nothing more than a weekend spent driving from San Diego to Hays, Kansas.

I had arranged with Holly and her roommate to share their apartment. Holly was a year ahead of me in her nursing courses, and she and her roommate lived on the second story of an old home that had been converted into a small apartment. In addition to having two bedrooms, this apartment had a small kitchen, one bathroom, a living room, and an attic. The tiny attic area would be my own personal space. It would also provide me with my first opportunity to learn how to improvise and develop ways to regulate temperature control because the attic had no heat or air-conditioning.

The attic was freezing cold in the blustery and snowy Kansas winters, and I could easily scrape frost off the interior walls. I learned to sleep with the clothes I planned to wear the next day tucked under my sheets and blankets at the foot of my bed to keep them warm. In the mornings, I would hurriedly grab these relatively warm clothes, run down the stairs to the bathroom, shut the door, and quickly turn on the hot-water tap of the tub. The steam from the hot water filling the tub would permeate the room, providing me with warmth and maintaining the warmth of the clothes I would put on. Every day I dreaded leaving that warm, tiny bathroom to return to my freezing room in the attic. Still, despite the attic being so cold in the winter and the hottest, most stifling place in the world during the summer months, it was cheap, and I managed to devise ways to keep as comfortable as possible. I had no way of knowing that these lessons learned from living in that attic would serve me well some twenty years later in the sands of Iraq.

When I arrived in Kansas, I knew I needed to surrender my green active-duty military identification card to military authorities on the date of its expiration. I visited a local Kansas recruiter and told that person I would like to remain on an active reserve status with the intent of becoming a commissioned officer in the Navy Nurse Corps upon graduating from the nursing program. The recruiter was thrilled, but unfortunately there were no active reserve navy drilling units located anywhere in western Kansas. The best the state had to offer was an army reserve unit that actively drilled right there in Hays.

Although I felt like I was betraying my strong and steadfast allegiance to the navy, I chose to enlist as an E-4 (the fourth enlisted rank; in the army this is corporal, whereas in the navy it is petty officer third class) in the U.S. Army Reserve. I saw this enlistment as simply an opportunity to remain on an active military status during the time I would be in school and nothing more than a means to an end. My monthly weekend drill time was spent working in the various hospitals, where I also completed my clinical training associated with the various specialty rotations of the university's nursing program. Everything was working out well the first few months, and from my personal perspective, being in the army was not so bad.

In the spring of 1981, eight months after joining the army, my reserve unit received orders to Fitzsimmons Army Medical Center in Colorado for its one week of intensive readiness training. This exercise was scheduled at the same time as my college spring break, and once again it appeared that everything was working out and that my status in the army was not interfering with my primary goal of obtaining my nursing degree.

As I waited with others in my army reserve unit to embark on our one-week training mission to Fitzsimmons, several seven-ton trucks rolled in. I was quickly issued basic army uniforms, which did not include any foul-weather or winter gear, and was harshly told, "Get your ass on the truck!" As we rode toward Colorado, the weather turned bitterly cold, and there was even snow on the ground. I was freezing, and without the proper gear that would protect me from the elements, I knew I was headed toward disaster and total misery. We had no tents, no berthing, no nothing other than the frozen, snowy mountainous ground on which to sleep. I could not help but reflect on all my dad had told me about that navy guarantee of always having a roof over your head and never having to sleep out on the open ground.

Immediately following that brutal, absolutely ridiculous experience—the true purpose of which still remains a mystery to me—I knew the army was definitely not for me. If this was an example of their slogan of the time, "Be All That You Can Be," I knew I could and would be much more.

As soon as I returned to Kansas, I called the navy recruiter in Topeka and told him I wanted out of the army reserve. I knew without a doubt that I would gladly drive however many miles I needed to so that I could be with a navy unit, and I told the recruiter, "Just get me out of the army now!" The recruiter was well aware that my ultimate goal was to be commissioned as a Navy Nurse Corps officer following nursing school and was happy to hear in my voice the passion I continued to have for the navy. He quickly processed my transfer request, and I was thrilled when I was informed that I was officially out of the army, back in the navy, and attached to a reserve unit in Wichita, Kansas.

To continue and maintain my active-duty military reserve status would require me to get up in the wee hours of the morning once a month to drive several hundred miles to meet up with my navy reserve unit. In addition, I would have to make numerous personal sacrifices not only to drill monthly in Wichita but also to execute the two weeks of annual readiness training held in San Diego. Drilling with the army may have been more convenient, but returning to the navy was like coming home again. I was back on familiar ground, wearing a navy uniform and communicating in navy lingo. (I was able to refer to the bathroom as the "head" rather than the "latrine" again!) I would continue drilling with this navy reserve unit until I graduated from nursing school, all the while feeling comforted and reassured that I was back where I belonged.

While attending Fort Hays University, I was required to obtain physical education course credits, so I enrolled in a running course. Running seemed to be a relatively easy activity, and I viewed at it as a relatively easy way to earn physical education credits. After all, how hard could it be to run a few hours a couple of days a week? Arriving at the first running class, I found I was the only female among a group of young men who were on the university's cross-country team. Whereas they had all enrolled in the course to create additional time in their schedules to continue training and to maintain their competitive edge, my intent was much less ambitious. Still, I was young and in reasonably good shape, and I loved being outdoors and believed I could make it through the course unscathed and with the required credits that would be applied toward my nursing degree.

Our class would meet as a group at a designated area, and our coach would tell us how many miles we were expected to run that day. We did not run circles on a smooth, oval, man-made asphalt track; our running assignment was to run on uneven, primitive trails, up and down hills, through fields, out in the middle of nowhere. The cross-country guys would always be well ahead of me; often, I could not even see them. There was no way I could keep up, and many times they would wait for me or would complete their required miles and circle back to where I was, just so I was not left out in the exposed terrain

with darkness quickly approaching. Their kind and compassionate
actions spurred me to begin running faster because I did not want
them to sacrifice their time and energy just to help ensure my own personal safety.

Before long these guys became my "running buddies." We
bonded as a group, always looking out for one another and motivating,
supporting, and encouraging each other to achieve our personal best.
The more I came to know them, and the more I ran, the more the passion for running seeped into my soul. The guys at Fort Hays University were very much there for me, motivating me to run farther and
faster, and I soon found that I was in love with running and that it had
become my own personal passion. Running provided me with a
release, a sense of freedom and control, and an opportunity to think
and put the various frustrations of life's happenings into perspective. It
gave me the sense of calm and serenity that I needed then and would
continue to need throughout my navy career.

The nursing program at Fort Hays University provided me with the
education, knowledge, and general nursing foundation I needed and
desired. I loved the science courses, and at my graduation in December 1982, I believed I was equipped with the medical and nursing
knowledge, tools, and skills that would help me perform as a qualified,
licensed registered nurse in the Navy Nurse Corps.

Before reporting to my first duty station where I would begin
functioning as a nurse, I was required to attend Officer Indoctrination
School (OIS) in Newport, Rhode Island. Following a brief visit with
my family in Pennsylvania, I reported to the OIS in February 1983.
Newport was bloody cold and would continue to be so for the next six
weeks.

Having been enlisted earlier and having endured nine weeks of
boot camp and recruit training, I found the demands of the OIS to be
small in comparison. Our days were spent marching on the grinder,
preparing for personnel and room inspections, and attending classes

where we received instruction specific to navy rules and regulations, traditions, customs, and leadership. I had already been there and done that, and much of what was required of us was already second nature to me.

I believe I would have enjoyed the OIS more had it not been for catching a nasty, lingering, energy-draining cold as a result of undergoing the "Buttercup experience." One of the first tasks we were to accomplish required us to be put into a building (the "Buttercup") that resembled a ship. As the building was flooded with the ice-cold water of Narragansett Bay, we were to work as a team in an attempt to save this simulated sinking ship. Being submerged in that bone-chilling February water of Newport was unbearable, and it significantly diminished my body's defenses against germs and viruses. Every day thereafter, I suffered from a constant runny nose, a sore throat, and a feeling of being miserable all over. I was determined from that day on never to choose to go to a place that was so cold. The weather and climate of an area would remain an important factor for me and would often be how I would choose future duty stations throughout my navy career.

On 1 April 1983, I was commissioned as an ensign in the U.S. Navy Nurse Corps and received orders to Naval Hospital, San Diego. I was assigned to an open-bay, enlisted men–only general surgical ward, a large, open area where all the hospital beds were lined up next to each other and all could be viewed from the nurses' station. I soon discovered that what I had learned in nursing school did not completely prepare me for all that I would encounter working as a nurse in the Navy Nurse Corps.

I was the only nurse assigned on the evening shift and had only two corpsmen to assist me with patient care in this very active thirty-six-bed unit. We worked hard. Many of the patients in this unit were acutely ill and unstable and required intensive and extensive procedures and ministrations. The administration of intravenous total parental nutrition, maintenance of central venous pressure lines, numerous dressing changes, respiratory care, and other treatments critical for the care of fresh postoperative patients were common and constant. In addition to administering patient care and teaching and supervising corpsmen—specifically in how to provide the needed care—the nurse was also responsible for various administrative details inherent with patient-care documentation and the general management of the ward.

Because this was an open-bay ward, many of the patients who had progressed in their recovery could easily see when one of their shipmates was in need, and they quickly offered their assistance with such simple tasks as filling water pitchers. They also served as much-needed extra eyes and ears and would be quick to alert us if one of their shipmates was in distress. It was a beautiful example of teamwork and of how the navy truly does take care of its own. I loved working on this ward. I was guided in my developing role as a practicing nurse by my charge nurse, Cdr. Janet Kozlowski, whom I had previously met when she was teaching at the Naval School of Health Sciences (NSHS), San Diego.

Despite my love of working on this surgical floor, I continued to be intrigued with the ICU and the post-anesthetic care unit (PACU), where patients' conditions were even more critical and the treatments were more highly specialized and intricate. As a result of the active support of several wonderful senior nurses, including Commander Kozlowski, Cdr. Anne Rawley (area coordinator), Capt. Maggie Donahue (director of nursing service), Lt. Cdr. Eugene Lujan (recovery room charge nurse), and Cdr. Arlene Southerland (ICU and PACU charge nurse), I was reassigned to the staff of the PACU, even though I was a mere ensign. I was even further cross-trained to deliver care in the ICU. In addition to learning valuable skills and receiving tremendous experience in hands-on patient care, I wrote two papers specific to hypothermia (subnormal body temperatures) and extubation (removal of a tube from the trachea) criteria that were published.

Because the PACU/recovery room required personnel with highly specialized skills and advanced knowledge in order to function with proficiency and authority, I decided—then a lieutenant (junior grade)—to write a point paper outlining why I believed the recovery room should become an official designated subspecialty for navy nurses. After it was forwarded through the chain of command at San Diego, my paper came to the attention of Rear Adm. Marianne Stratton, director of the Navy Nurse Corps. During a visit to the San Diego area for a conference, Admiral Stratton came to visit me to discuss the various points outlined in this paper. Ultimately, the navy would approve the designation of this subspecialty code for nurses throughout the Navy Nurse Corps.

In September 1986, I was frocked as a lieutenant, and my tour of duty at Naval Hospital, San Diego, was quickly drawing to its end. Having had so many positive experiences as a Navy Nurse Corps officer while at San Diego, I decided that leaving the corps for a civilian career was not an option. All I wanted to do was pick another place that was warm and to charge on, growing, developing, and being all that I could be as a navy nurse.

I was due for an overseas tour of duty and had filled in various overseas duty stations on my "dream sheet" (my list of preferred stations) without being truly aware of their exact locations. When the duty-assignment manager told me that I would be going to the Philippines, it was only then that I looked at a map and thought, "Hmmm, that's pretty far from here, but it looks to be a tropical place, and I am sure the weather will be warm."

Prior to shipping out to the Philippines in 1986, I went back to Fleetwood to be with my family. It was around Christmas, and it would be a very special time for me, filled with many cherished memories of baking cookies with my mother, my sister, and my Grandmother Ruff. My Grandmother Ruff retrieved an aged bottle of homemade wine that had been packaged in 1980 in an old-fashioned Log Cabin syrup bottle by my grandfather just prior to his death. When my grandmother gave me this highly prized possession as a parting gift, she said, "You need to have a little toast." Shortly after this visit home, my grandmother would have a debilitating stroke, and this, along with

worsening symptoms associated with Parkinson's disease, would require her to enter a nursing care facility. That visit would be my last at
Grandmother Ruff's home. Prior to catching my flight to the Philippines, I opened that bottle of wine in honor of my grandparents and
shared it with Shirley and Gordon Cornell during a quiet bon voyage
dinner.

Arriving at Clark Air Force Base, I was reunited with Lt. Carolyn Shaw,
a navy nurse with whom I had been stationed at San Diego. She would
serve as my sponsor. Despite being December, the weather was hot
and muggy, and I knew it would become even hotter and more humid
as the months passed. Traveling to Subic Bay and then on to Cubi
Point where the Naval Hospital was located, I looked out the bus window and saw neighborhoods and dwellings that reminded me of the
poor, dilapidated neighborhoods of Tijuana, Mexico.

I did not know upon arriving at this duty station that it would
become my favorite in my twenty-five-year naval career. Reunited with
many friends and colleagues with whom I had been stationed in San
Diego, including Cdr. Alicia Deprima, who was serving as the director
of nursing service, I felt almost like I was being stationed at an annex
of the Naval Hospital in San Diego. I was thousands of miles from California, yet, being surrounded by so many good friends, I felt as
though I had never left. We would work hard and play hard, and they
would be there for me when I was notified of the death of my Grandfather McKently in June 1987, followed by the sudden death of my
father in March 1988. It was difficult being so far away from home
when these losses occurred, but my friends, my overseas adopted family, provided me the comfort and support to help me work through the
grieving process.

Initially assigned to a male medical-surgical open-bay ward at U.S.
Naval Hospital, Subic Bay, Philippine Islands, I would eventually move
to the three-bed ICU where I would serve as charge nurse. Many of
the patients we received had conditions so critical that they could not

be transported stateside and would be in our care for many months. In addition to learning and growing in the field of intensive care nursing, I would also learn how to care for patients with an array of tropical diseases and conditions—tuberculosis, tetany, malaria, and dengue, for example—not commonly seen in stateside facilities. I will never forget the sight of worms crawling out the ends of endotracheal tubes or finding worms stuck to the tip of the suction catheter I had been using to clear a patient's airway.

We always had something to see or do on and around the base when we were not working. One of our favorite activities was to rent a ski boat and spend hours water-skiing, boating, or simply relaxing as the boat drifted beneath clear blue skies. Travel opportunities were abundant. I had the opportunity to travel five times to Hong Kong, China (including Beijing), Singapore, Jakarta, and Australia, and I was able to experience a two-week backpacking and elephant-tracking adventure in Chiang Mai, Thailand.

Periodically, the hospital staff would go out on what we called "jungle excursions." Leaving a skeleton crew behind on the hospital wards to attend to any in-house issues concerning patient care, we would go into the jungle of the Philippines, set up tents, and perform mass casualty drills. U.S. Marines and Navy helicopter pilots would join us in these drills, and simulated patients would be brought to us for triage and care. It was definitely a different environment and type of medicine from what I had experienced while working on the hospital wards or in the ICU, but the knowledge I gained would be of great help to me.

In July 1989, I received orders to Naval Hospital, Camp Pendleton, California. Capt. Elizabeth Muszynski, director of nursing service, assigned me to work in the ICU even though my first choice was the PACU. Still, I was thrilled when I discovered my charge nurse was Cdr. Annie Mulligan, a navy nurse and a marathon runner. I had heard of her and had wanted to meet her. Although I had continued fulfilling my passion for running while in the Philippines, a major desire of mine was to learn how to run marathons. My assignment and meeting of Commander Mulligan seemed destined.

Annie would indeed teach me to run marathons, and I would run several marathon events throughout California and later in other states across the country. When Annie departed with orders to Naval Hospital, Oakland, and despite being simply a lieutenant at the time, I became charge nurse of the ICU. Blessed with a wonderful staff of ensigns, lieutenants, and corpsmen who were experienced, knowledgeable, and highly skilled, the ICU was well staffed and efficient, and it offered the highest possible caliber of patient care. My nursing supervisors, Cdr. Linda Massey and Cdr. Leslie Robinson, trusted my abilities as both nurse and leader and allowed me full and final reign of decisions specific to the ICU's management.

On 21 January 1991, my thirty-third birthday, I was informed that I would be deployed on board the hospital ship USNS *Mercy* (T-AH 19) for temporary additional duty. The *Mercy* had deployed in August 1990 in support of Operation Desert Storm. By early 1991, fighting between the coalition forces and Saddam Hussein's Republican Guard loomed close on the horizon.

Arriving on board the ship and being one of the later arrivals, I was assigned to an open-bay berthing area. Where I was berthed mattered little to me, for I was simply excited and eager to have the opportunity to be in the action, supporting our military forces in the best way I knew how. My primary work assignment would be a sub-unit of the triage area dedicated to major-trauma victims who might be brought on board via helicopters. Ens. Mike DiBonaventura was assigned to this area with me as my staff nurse, and neither he nor I could have ever imagined that the next time we would see one another would be twelve years later in the sands of Kuwait.

When my services were not needed in the triage area, I worked in the ICU. Fortunately, the *Mercy* did not receive numerous casualties of war during Operation Desert Storm. Also known as the Gulf War, that operation was quick and precise, and it resulted in very few personnel wounded in battle. With the exception of a few American and coalition fighting troops injured in accidents, the majority of those for whom we provided care were our own prisoners of war who were brought back on board the *Mercy* when we sailed into Bahrain.

Although my shipboard tour was brief, about three weeks in duration, I loved everything about the *Mercy*. We were not overloaded with patients, yet the training we received was invaluable. Commander Deprima, with whom I had been stationed twice previously, guided us in our efforts and work. Her trusting leadership style was a perfect match to my conscientious, thorough, and independent work approach.

Returning to the Naval Hospital, Camp Pendleton, I resumed my position as charge nurse of the ICU. Life returned to normal; I worked hard, continued running marathons, socialized with friends, and pursued a variety of other outdoor interests. Soon, as is the case with all military installations, personnel staff changes occurred at the Naval Hospital, and I found myself working for a supervisor who was a micromanager. This supervisor, unlike Commander Robinson, did not trust my judgment or decision-making process. Despite this disparity, I continued making sound, independent decisions specific to the management of the ICU that were not always in concert with the desires of my supervisor. As a result, I received a less-than-favorable annual fitness report (FITREP). I was miserable and believed this FITREP would squash any chances of future promotion. I even thought it might prove to be the demise of my career as a navy nurse. I adamantly disagreed with my evaluation and steadfastly refused to sign it.

Fortunately, my career would soon be saved by the arrival of the new director of nursing service, then-Captain Deprima. She thoroughly researched the circumstances surrounding the various decisions I had made specific to the ICU, and the FITREP was revised. The subtle negative verbiage contained in the report was removed, and I happily signed it just prior to leaving to execute my next set of orders to the NSHS, San Diego.

In November 1991, I reported to the NSHS, where I would be assigned as an instructor at the Hospital Corps School. I had always wanted to teach there and saw it as a way to pay back all that had been given to me as a young enlisted sailor. This was my opportunity to give to the young folks, the navy's future, just as so many had given to me when I had first started my naval career. Watching my students grow, learn, and discover their skills and talents was tremendously fulfilling.

Still, the position was also strenuous; I found myself assisting these young people in solving an array of personal issues, ranging from severe financial difficulties to delicate marital, family, and relationship problems.

As my tour at the NSHS drew to a close, I found that I had achieved all of my initial career goals and more. I was as clinically experienced in the field of ICU as I could be, I had fulfilled my dream of teaching at the Hospital Corps School, I had been given the opportunity to travel throughout the world, and I had met and become very close friends with many wonderful people. I had even been selected and promoted to the rank of lieutenant commander, the rank I needed to achieve in order to retire and receive the maximum retirement benefits for my service. Still, I believed there was more to do, and I began thinking about what I wanted to do next.

Reflecting on my days in nursing school at Fort Hays University, I remembered a time when various advanced practiced nurses came to the school and spoke to us about their particular specialties. I distinctly remembered a nurse anesthetist being one of the speakers. She told us how her role incorporated pharmacology with the patient's physiological state, plus patient care. I knew even then that the role of a nurse anesthetist was a perfect match for what I desired most, and I began researching the prospect of attending the navy's education program for nurse anesthetists.

Completing my student candidate's packet for nurse anesthesia school was extremely time consuming, requiring several months to develop. It was comparable to developing and writing a master's thesis, or at least it seemed so at the time. I developed the most comprehensive, straightforward, and precise packet I was capable of creating. Guiding me in my efforts were Capt. Sherry Henderson, a family practice physician assigned to the NSHS, Cdr. Barb Ramsey, a fellow navy nurse, and Cdr. Anne Hanzel, who spent hours reviewing and editing several versions of my school packet. My diligent work, the support of my friends, and the letters of recommendation from Lt. Cdr. Judi Jo Johnson, Lt. Cdr. Karin Lundgren, and Lt. Cdr. Julie Donahue Pearson, all of whom were certified registered nurse anesthetists (CRNAs), paid off. On 21 January 1994, my thirty-sixth birthday, I was informed that I had been selected for the nurse anesthesia program. I was due to report to the NSHS, Bethesda, Maryland, six months later.

About that time, the navy's nurse anesthesia education program became affiliated with Georgetown University's CRNA program, and it would prove to be the most grueling and relentless experience I had ever encountered. My days and nights were totally consumed with attending lectures, studying, writing papers, and performing dissections in the anatomy laboratory. The year of didactic instruction at Georgetown University was brutal, but with the help of my fellow students and study partners—Lt. Cdr. Tamara Martin and Cdr. Debra Yarema—I completed it successfully and advanced to phase two of the program. This phase consisted of eighteen months of additional training and supervised clinical practice at the Naval Medical Center (NMC), Portsmouth, Virginia, and at various civilian hospitals in the southern Virginia Tidewater area. Being exposed to other nurse anesthesia providers in civilian facilities demonstrated to me the vast difference between anesthesia practice in the navy and the practice within the civilian community. The emphasis for the navy's nurse anesthetist was to function independently as the only anesthesia provider, making sound, quick judgments and taking immediate action no matter what the situation or environment might encompass.

Two weeks prior to graduating in February 1997, my mother experienced a global ischemic attack, and she, along with others in my family, was unable to attend the graduation ceremony. Concerned about my mother but happy about reaching my goal, I graduated with a Master of Science degree in nursing anesthesia and reported for assignment to the National Naval Medical Center (NNMC), Bethesda.

Being in Maryland brought me the closest to my family's home that I had ever been in my navy career, and I was pleased. My youngest cousin, Kathy, was in her third year of fighting breast cancer and had recently come out of remission. Her cancer had metastasized, and I wanted to be close to home, ready to help her as much as possible. Now that I was in Maryland, I would be able to go home quickly.

In April 1997, while visiting my family in rural Pennsylvania, I received a call from Capt. P. Jan Chandler, a navy surgeon, and Capt. Carol Cooper, a navy lawyer. These neighbors of mine in Maryland had been collecting my mail and watching over my residence while I was away. I had been waiting eagerly to hear word about my nurse anesthesia certification results. When Jan informed me that I had indeed passed the certification board's testing requirement and was a true CRNA, I was extremely happy. It was even more meaningful to me because I had the opportunity to celebrate this accomplishment at my childhood home surrounded by my family.

I would continue to remain assigned to the NNMC from 1997 until 2000, all the while making frequent trips home to Pennsylvania on weekends and extended holidays. This three-year tour of duty was enjoyable. I steered clear of the ever-changing political climate of the day and concentrated on learning, practicing, and refining my skill as a CRNA.

While at NNMC, I was also assigned collaterally as the chief nurse anesthetist for the hospital ship USNS *Comfort* (T-AH 20). In this position, my sole responsibility was to ensure that the ship's anesthesia department was ready for any contingency, whether it was in response to war or a national disaster or for humanitarian purposes. This collateral assignment to the *Comfort* would be the first of many more shipboard nursing experiences I would encounter as my career in the navy continued.

# 4

# ANCHORS AWEIGH

In June 1997 the USNS *Comfort* pulled out of Baltimore Harbor on a humanitarian mission called the Baltic Challenge. We would be deployed for more than a month to several Baltic countries and would see many sites none of us had ever witnessed before. The experiences we would have—clinically, socially, and culturally—would be incredible and would reside in our memories forever.

At one of the first ports in Lithuania where we dropped anchor, a woman ran up to the ship and cried, "Please! Please, help me! Help my child!" Her fifteen-year-old son had a large tumor growing from the back of his head. The extensive, delicate neurological surgery to correct the deformity would take close to nine hours to perform. I felt privileged to be involved in this procedure. The *Comfort* had been outfitted with the best medical equipment and advanced telecommunications capabilities, allowing us to transmit computed axial tomography (CAT) and magnetic resonance imaging (MRI) scans to the Radiology Department at NNMC for expert review and analysis. This ability to send and receive images and medical testing between ship and shore was a first; we were making history. The standard of care enhanced by the telecommunications capabilities initiated on board the *Comfort* during the Baltic Challenge set the standard for future shipboard medical practice.

Returning to NNMC, I continued to work as a staff CRNA in the operating room. My cousin Kathy was receiving extensive treatment in her battle against breast cancer, including stem cell transplant. She was hospitalized in Philadelphia; I would work in Bethesda during the week and travel to Pennsylvania to assist her on the weekends. Being the only medical professional in my family, I was looked to for explanations why certain treatments and procedures were being performed, what to expect as a result of those treatments and procedures, and what treatment choices might be best.

In August 1999 I was notified that I would be assigned to Fleet Surgical Team Eight based at Little Creek Naval Amphibious Base, Norfolk, Virginia. Before reporting to the surgical team, I was provided an opportunity to deploy on the aircraft carrier USS *Roosevelt* (CVN 71) for a month of training and hands-on practice at sea. I thoroughly enjoyed being on the carrier, and I loved practicing the art of anesthesia in a true navy operational setting. I would soon discover, though, that aircraft carriers are 100 percent different from amphibious ships, on which I would also be deployed.

In April 2000 I reported to Little Creek. As the only anesthesia provider to be deployed on various amphibious ships for durations of up to six months, I knew I needed to be as knowledgeable, responsible, and highly skilled as possible. My number one priority was the care of the sailors and marines attached to the ship.

The differences between the amphibious ship and the *Roosevelt* were readily apparent. Whereas the aircraft carriers received generous supplies and equipment immediately upon request, I discovered that obtaining supplies and equipment for the amphibious ships took diligence, perseverance, and even some scrounging. Compensation for that which we were unable to acquire in supplies or equipment would require creativity, imagination, and the ability to efficiently use or modify whatever supplies we had on hand to get the job done. This lesson would serve me well a mere three years later when I would find myself providing patient care with even fewer supplies and even more archaic anesthesia equipment than what was available on board the amphibious ships.

Berthing on board the various ships would also vary. The carriers were equipped with individual staterooms, but the berthing on board the amphibious ships, especially the USS *Saipan* (LHA 2), proved to be a different story. As one of the older multipurpose amphibious ships, she had not been fully retrofitted to accommodate female sailors. The small group of us assigned to the ship was berthed in one hallway, and we all shared one small head that was designated "for females only." Officer staterooms were shared; my roommate was a lieutenant female helicopter pilot.

During my six-month Mediterranean cruise aboard the *Saipan*, I worked with a dynamic group of medical and nursing professionals, including Lt. Alex Matthews, surgeon; Lt. Mike Picio, family practice physician; and Lt. Gene Trusdale, operating room nurse. The corpsmen were also well trained, hardworking, and eager to provide the best patient care possible. Our deployment in the year 2000 brought many challenges, some surgical and some environmental. We encountered some storms so fierce that our commanding officer likened them to *The Perfect Storm*. He often remarked that the conditions we encountered during that cruise were worse than any he had experienced in nine previous deployments.

While we were meeting the challenges of working and living on board the USS *Saipan* as she was tossed violently about by the storms, we were notified of the 12 October 2000 bombing of the USS *Cole* (DDG 67) while she was docked in Yemen to take on fuel. Killing seventeen young sailors and injuring thirty-nine others, this terrorist attack brought changes to our ship's itinerary, heightened security to ports of call, and created a need to relocate scheduled training missions. Unrest between Palestine and Israel was also occurring during this time, and instead of docking at an Israeli port, a plan that had been in place for more than a year and a location where the marines had rou-tinely performed military exercises and maneuvers, the *Saipan* went to Croatia. Despite this abrupt change of the ship's course, the Marine Expeditionary Force (MEF) was able to conduct an outstanding train-ing experience, and Croatia would soon replace Israel as the location for future overseas MEF exercises.

During that Mediterranean cruise, I became acutely aware of the heightened unrest and threat of terrorism in the Middle East. Another nine months would elapse before I would know just how unsettled the world was and how terrorism would impact every citizen of the United States of America.

In June 2001, Fleet Surgical Team Eight, to which I was still assigned, was attached to the USS *Wasp* (LHD 1). We were docked at one of the many piers at the U.S. Naval Base, Norfolk, Virginia, and as crew members we were in the process of preparing her workups and sea tri-als for an upcoming six-month routine and scheduled Mediterranean cruise. For close to three months our days were typical, and the start of 11 September 2001 seemed to be no different, other than calling my mother to wish her a happy seventy-seventh birthday.

On learning of the 11 September 2001 terrorist attacks on the World Trade Center and on the Pentagon, all shipboard military per-sonnel were mandated to report immediately to their assigned ships. Thousands of sailors and marines residing in the Tidewater and Hamp-ton Roads area surrounding Norfolk scrambled to get their affairs in order, pack their seabags, say good-bye to their loved ones, and make their way expeditiously to their assigned ships. Snarled in what seemed like a never-ending line of traffic, compounded by an additional delay as we were carefully scrutinized by the base's heavily armed guards before being allowed on base, I spent four long hours trying to reach the ship, which was a mere twenty miles from my home.

Once aboard the *Wasp*, we were told to "hold tight." No one knew whether we would deploy or hold fast or what our role might be as the devastation of the attacks began to unfold hour by hour and the reality of the events began to sink in. As night approached, we were told to go home, "stand by," and be ready to return to the ship at a moment's notice. From September until December 2001, I continued to maintain a personal state of readiness, equipped and prepared to report for duty, no matter what that duty might entail.

In November, while still attached to the *Wasp,* I received orders to report to Naval Medical Center, Portsmouth, Virginia, in January 2002. My replacement, Lt. Bob Hawkins, had reported to the *Wasp,* and after a thorough turnover was completed, I had an opportunity to deploy in a temporary-additional-duty status to the USS *George Washington* (CVN 73) prior to executing my permanent-change-of-station orders to Naval Hospital, Portsmouth. I thoroughly enjoyed being deployed for three weeks on the carrier, and it provided me with additional experience in operational medicine, something I loved and knew I would never have an opportunity to experience as a civilian CRNA.

Unfortunately, during this same period of time, my cousin Kathy's medical condition took a turn for the worse. During the Thanksgiving holidays of 2001, I had visited with her and expressed my love and gratitude to her for our unconditional "best friend" forty-year-long relationship. As I sat on board the *George Washington* somewhere in the wide-open, expansive Atlantic Ocean, I grew frustrated when I received her e-mail telling me she would be entering the hospital for what she expected to be her final days. For four very long days prior to returning to home port, I knew very little of Kathy's condition, and my sense of urgency to get back to Pennsylvania to be with her grew stronger with each passing hour.

Within hours after the *George Washington* pulled into port, I was on my way to Pennsylvania, where I would spend the next two weeks with Kathy at the hospital, caring for her, talking with her, and just being there for her. On our last day together, 31 December 2001, I told her how very much I loved her and said, "I don't have anything else that I feel I need to say that I haven't ever said to you. Is there any-thing you need to say to me?" Kathy then expressed her love for me and thanked me for everything I had done for her. "Will I ever see you again?" she asked. I looked at her and said, "Yep! I'll see you in heaven," to which she readily agreed.

Kathy's young life came to its tragic end a few hours later. Although her death hit me hard and I deeply grieved for her, I was also able to perceive and feel the tremendously positive impact she had had on me as I grew, matured, and set my sail on a life's course so radically different from her own. The memories I had of our times growing up together in Fleetwood and the love she had so freely and graciously given to me would remain with me, comforting my heart and making me smile as I charged forward determined to make every day and every experience truly count. Kathy's death at the age of forty heightened my awareness of my own mortality and made me even more deter-mined to live a full life, taking nothing for granted, cherishing each and every day, and doing everything in my power to help others.

In January 2002, I reported to NMC, Portsmouth. Now back at the facility where I had trained as an anesthesia student and was being reunited with friends and colleagues I had known for many years, I assumed my assigned position as a hospital staff CRNA. I continued administering anesthesia and providing care to a variety of active-duty personnel, retirees, and military dependents, each of whom required surgical intervention.

Navy Medical Department personnel were usually assigned to an operational platform as their primary billet, and their secondary billet was duty at a hospital or other military treatment facility. On being informed that my primary assignment was duty at the hospital (not an operational billet), I was very disappointed. I had served on board both of the navy's hospital ships, two amphibious ships, and two aircraft car-riers, and I believed I possessed real-world working knowledge, as well as a heck of a lot of operational medical/surgical experience. I had "been there, done that" and staunchly believed that my primary billet should be an operational one, not the stable, routine, and highly regulated stateside military treatment facility billet to which I was assigned.

The world had entered into unsettled times; military action was being conducted in Afghanistan in support of Operation Enduring Freedom, and other troops were beginning to deploy to Kuwait in support of Operation Iraqi Freedom. If needed to provide surgical support for these fighting forces, whether it was assignment on board a ship or on the battlefield, I wanted to be there and could only do so if my primary assignment was an operational billet.

It would take several months of making numerous phone calls and constantly petitioning my chain of command for me to finally be assigned to an operational billet as my primary duty. In October 2002, I was notified that my primary billet would be the Second Force Service Support Group (FSSG), and I was thrilled. There was no way for me to know then just how much that assignment would change my life forever.

# 5

## DEPLOYMENT

On 22 January 2003, the commander of the Second FSSG came to NMC, Portsmouth, to talk with those of us assigned to his unit. After he spoke to our group of approximately eighty for more than ninety minutes, we were all very motivated and ready to go. At the end of his address, he said, "We have already picked the twenty-six people who will be deploying imminently, and I would like those people, and you know who you are, to come forward. The rest of you can go back to work."

Not having been previously notified that I was one of the twenty-six chosen, I left the commander's briefing feeling disappointed. Since being assigned to the Second FSSG, I had diligently prepared for operational deployment, spending numerous hours with my family and friends to make comprehensive arrangements specific to my life affairs. I knew everything was in order. Still, I had no choice but to accept that my deployment with the Second FSSG was not meant to be. I left the briefing, proceeded to the retirement office, and obtained the required forms and checklists needed to begin the physical exam process for retirement. My request for retirement from the navy after twenty-five years of service had been previously approved, and my official retirement date was 1 August 2003.

That evening, I called Jeryl. She was thrilled to hear that I was not among the twenty-six chosen to deploy and just kept saying "Thank God, thank God." Those same sentiments were echoed in additional phone calls I made to friends. Still, I could not shake my feelings of disappointment. I wanted to go to Kuwait and then on to Iraq. I wanted to be there to apply my skills and to support our troops in the way I knew I was trained.

As directed by the commander, I had gone back to work the following day and resumed my assigned duties as a staff nurse anesthetist. Twenty-three January started in the usual way in the operating room at NMC Portsmouth. We had several surgical cases scheduled and were meeting with our assigned patients prior to taking them into the operating room. While I was talking with my patient in the preoperative hold area, Cdr. Pamela Giza, associate director for surgical support, arrived. I could tell by the look on her face that something was up and that this day was not going to be a typical one for me.

Intuitively, I knew what she was going to tell me, and for a moment, my heart sank. At the same time, I was elated. Since 11 September 2001, I had mentally prepared for this deployment, and I wanted very much to go. When she told me I was definitely going to be deployed with the Second FSSG, I felt a mixture of emotions: happy, sad, fearful, concerned, and excited. I did not know precisely how to feel, and I had no idea what to expect.

Once again I called my sister. Hearing the news of my inevitable and immediate deployment, she just started crying. She knew this deployment would be very different from my previous ones, and she deeply feared for my safety.

My mom, on the other hand, kept saying to me, "You'll do fine; everything will work out," the same words of encouragement she had spoken to me thousands of times throughout my life. This time, however, I wanted her to express more. I desperately needed her to comprehend that this deployment would be different from all the others in my career and far beyond the challenge of a simple math test. I was being deployed to the ground of a country with whom we would soon be at war, and I would be in harm's way. This deployment would be a dangerous and brutal journey with no guarantees. Believing it was also one from which I might never return, I wanted my mother to be aware of all the preparations I had made in the event of my death. More important, I needed her to know how I appreciated everything she had given and sacrificed for me throughout my forty-five years of life and to comprehend fully the deep, profound, and resolute love I felt for her. Nothing else would comfort my soul or provide the sense of peace I craved.

Despite my daily phone conversations with my mother during the seven days prior to leaving, nothing I said seemed to sink in. She continued to end each call with her famous reassurance. I grew weary of our conversations and frustrated with my inability to communicate my most urgent need and desire.

By the eve of my deployment, I had become mentally and emotionally exhausted from attending to the myriad details associated with this upcoming deployment that could easily be my final life's journey. I called Jeryl and began to cry. The reality of my leaving, perhaps for the last time, had finally hit me. Everything was in order except the assurance that would come only with my mother's understanding of the danger and uncertainty I was facing. I told Jeryl, "I don't want Mom to tell me for the zillionth time, 'You'll be fine; everything will work out.' I need her to understand where I am going and that I might never come back." Jeryl responded, "I know, Cheryl. Let me call Mom, and I'll get back to you."

To this day, I have no idea what Jeryl said to my mother, but later that night when I called her, Mom refrained from offering those same worn-out words I had grown so tired of hearing. Instead, she spoke words I had so longed to hear, words that indicated she finally understood the true gravity of this perilous journey on which I was about to embark. Being able to tell her how much I loved her and believing she now heard me and fully understood gave me the sense of peace I had been seeking. I did not know then, nor would I know for several weeks, that Mom's inability to comprehend was not a result of either

her eternal-optimist personality or denial. Instead, it was a result of progressive dementia.

That night, after talking with Jeryl and Mom, I continued to experience a quiet sense of calmness and peace. For months, I had planned and prepared for this deployment. Everything—from when and how many tampons I would need to have sent to me, to where I wanted to be buried—had been carefully planned and reviewed with my sister. I had turned down the thermostat and cleaned my home. My neighbors had agreed to watch my property. I had done everything I could do for my sister, who would be the one to take care of any loose ends. My primary concern was not for myself or for my own safety; my worry was for those who might be burdened with my personal affairs if I never returned.

We were told to be at the hospital at 3 AM on 29 January. I arrived with my two seabags, one of them empty and the other packed tight. We had been given guidelines as to what to take, but I knew that everything I took with me I would need to carry. The empty seabag would be filled with gear that would be issued to us once we arrived at the staging base at Camp Lejeune, North Carolina. Knowing that I would be required to carry both seabags, one on my front and one on my back, I established my priorities and packed the bare minimum: uniforms, clothes, and toiletries. I was depending on my family to help me replenish my supplies of tampons, toothpaste, shampoo, soap, gum, and even jellybeans.

Approximately eighty of us waited to be loaded onto two buses. The original twenty-six mentioned by the Second FSSG commander only a week earlier had obviously increased. As I would realize later, this was simply the first example of the many times that what we were told the first time around would not always hold true.

Without fanfare, we began boarding the Bluebird school buses. As I boarded, I was handed my medical and dental records, Geneva Convention card, and two dog tags. I attached one of these dog tags to my seabag, and I laced the other onto my left boot as we were directed to do. I also had the original dog tags that had been issued to me twenty-five years ago when I was in boot camp; those tags I wore proudly around my neck. I thought it ironic that I should wear those same dog tags at both the beginning and the very end of my career.

I sat on the bus and watched families say their good-byes before boarding, and I wondered what it was like for them. Although I had no family to say good-bye to at the curb, my good friend and colleague Tamara "Tam" Cross Martin, whom I had known since nurse anesthesia school, was there to wish me well. Tam was assigned to Fleet Hospital Five, Portsmouth, and believed she would also soon be deploying to Iraq. I looked forward to the prospect of seeing her in Iraq, yet I also hoped she would not be required to go.

The four-hour bus ride to the U.S. Marine Corps base at Camp Lejeune was cramped and quiet. All were tired and preoccupied with their own thoughts. I sat with a man named Steve, a family practice physician who was stationed at the Oceana Naval Air Station clinic in Virginia Beach. We were wedged into a bus designed for transporting small children to and from school. The seats were small and uncomfortable and offered very little legroom. Steve's legs were bent up into his torso, and mine were extended into the aisle. It was impossible to find a position of comfort that would be conducive to napping, so Steve and I talked.

We soon discovered we had many things in common, including our home state of Pennsylvania. He had a sister who lived in Oley Valley, where I had attended school throughout the twelve years of my primary education. He was wonderful company, and I thoroughly enjoyed our "gabfest" as we made our way south to North Carolina. Little did I know at that time that Steve and I would remain together throughout our Iraqi deployment and would even ride in the same bus seats from our last campsite in Kuwait to the Kuwait International Airport, where we would begin the final leg of our journey home.

Arriving at the sprawling Marine Corps base around 9 AM, we were directed to a large room where we began filling out paperwork, such as notification of next of kin. Dog tags were also being issued to those who did not already have them. Each person had a total of three tags per person—one to be worn around the neck, one to be worn on a boot, and one to be fastened to the seabag. Our records were reviewed, and we received last-minute immunizations. A lot of down-time was spent completing paperwork, being briefed on an anticipated time line of events, and attending to last-minute details.

We received our room assignments, and I had the good fortune of being assigned with Lt. Cdr. Kelly James and Lt. Maria Norbeck, two operating room nurses with whom I had previously worked. Our barracks were cockroach infested, and the room was absolutely filthy. The cockroaches remained alive and well despite our attempt to kill them by spraying the room every third morning with Raid. We began to believe the roaches were wearing gas masks!

Although the barracks room to which we were assigned was less than ideal, I intuitively knew these stateside living conditions were nowhere near as dismal as what we would be facing once we arrived in the desert. I was just thankful to have been assigned with two benevolent, considerate, and optimistic women with whom I would be able to join forces to make it through this first leg of our journey. We quickly became a "battle buddy family," and their safety and comfort became just as important to me as my own.

We spent the day after our arrival acquiring our war gear. We literally went through a warehouse with shopping carts, loading each with a sleeping bag, liner, flak jacket, helmet, poncho, field jacket, Alice pack (an olive drab–colored backpack whose name is an acronym for *a*ll-purpose *l*ightweight *i*ndividual *c*arrying *e*quipment), web belt, canteens, and more. We were issued two sets of mission-oriented protective posture (MOPP) clothing and gear, with one gas mask and two gas mask filters. MOPP clothing consisted of a protective hood, battle-dress overgarment, overboots, and butyl rubber gloves. In the event of a chemical attack, this clothing, along with our gas mask, would protect us against nuclear, biological, and chemical contamination on the battlefield, or so we were told. All we could do was hope that the gear's protection theory was true.

We were also issued two empty ammunition magazines, pistol-cleaning gear, and holster. We completed a data card containing the serial number of our assigned 9-mm pistol. This card would be used to check out the pistol for the purpose of firing it on the practice shooting range while we waited in Camp Lejeune. Our ammunition and pistol would not be fully issued to us until the morning we departed for Kuwait.

The impossibility of fitting all the issued gear into the one empty seabag we had brought quickly became apparent. We had no other choice but to discard many personal items from our second seabag in order to make everything fit. Our war gear was our number one priority, for it was also our survival gear.

Three days after arriving at Camp Lejeune, we watched the television and were stunned by the images of the space shuttle Columbia disintegrating as it made its reentry into the earth's atmosphere. Here we were, a nation on the brink of war. We had a plan and total faith in the leaders of the United States. We believed we had the power, the ingenuity, and the technology to defeat our enemy. Still, as we watched the lives of those brave astronauts end in a fiery blaze, we began to have doubts. Fear for our own lives and the lives of our shipmates increased. Because I had aspired to be an astronaut throughout my youth and adolescence and had maintained a keen interest in the U.S. space program, the loss of these lives was especially tragic for me.

During those seventeen days at Camp Lejeune, I spent a lot of time packing and repacking my gear, working out in the gym, attending lectures, and practicing shooting my pistol on the range. I also spent hours breaking down that pistol into five parts in an attempt to refine my pistol-cleaning skill. Once we arrived in Kuwait, we would be required to clean our pistol daily, for we knew that the sand and dust of the desert could easily cause our weapons to jam or misfire. Each time I cleaned this weapon, I thought, "Will I truly be able to use this pistol to kill another human being?" It was a question for which I had no firm answer, at least not at that time. When I looked at this pistol, I knew it might be the only thing that would determine whether I would live or die. It had the power not only to take the life of another but also to end my own. Although I did not know whether I could take the life of another, I did know that if I faced the prospect of being captured, I would use my pistol to kill myself before I would become a prisoner of war. I had already made this decision before leaving my home.

At times, a group of us would get together to practice putting on our gas masks and MOPP gear. We used practice sets of MOPP gear for this exercise because the protective integrity of the gear was good for only a few days once the special seal and wrapping were removed. We soon became proficient, able to don the cumbersome hood, over-garment, boots, gloves, and mask within four minutes.

I also received intensive instruction specific to the field anesthesia equipment I would be using. Cdr. Mike Harrison, an anesthesiologist assigned to the Second FSSG, took me over to the base's Naval Hospital, where a replica of the field anesthesia machine and a small portable vaporizer were maintained. I was unfamiliar with this equipment, so Mike showed me how to assemble and disassemble it. Knowing that time was of the essence and could be the determining factor between saving or losing the life of a soldier once we were on the battlefield, I practiced and practiced assembling this equipment, both in light and in darkness. Eventually, I was able to master the equipment's assembly in slightly more than six minutes.

We were constantly being told that water would be scarce once we reached Kuwait and Iraq. I decided it would be more important to drink whatever water we would be issued rather than to use it to bathe. As a result of this information about the scarcity of water, combined with additional information about the ferocity and abundance of sand flies in the desert, I decided to get my first "marine barber haircut." It was horrible and very short. I remember thinking how embarrassed I would be for my family to see me looking like a little boy and only hoped the war would last long enough for it to grow in before I returned home.

I soon grew tired of waiting, filling my days with redundant drills, exercise, and lectures. I wanted to move on, and I was ready. I felt much the same as a racing greyhound must feel waiting to come out of the starting gates.

Throughout the week of 9–15 February, we heard rumors that we would be leaving by the end of the week. On Thursday, 13 February, we received definite word that we would be boarding a flight to Kuwait on Saturday. We had little left to do to prepare for our departure. Our clothes were washed and packed along with our war gear. We were ready. To celebrate the news of our departure, we went out to dine on Mexican food at a restaurant in town. As the beer and margaritas flowed, we all wondered when, if ever, we would have another opportunity to be surrounded by friends while savoring the food and drink of an American restaurant.

As it turned out, because 15 through 17 February was a three-day liberty weekend for military personnel in honor of Presidents' Day, we were ordered to check out of the barracks on Friday. This created a problem, though, because those of us from Portsmouth really had no place to go. Fortunately, Lt. Fleming French, an operating room nurse stationed at Camp Lejeune, graciously opened her house to Kelly, Maria, and me just so we would have a place to rest our heads for a few hours. Other local military families also opened their doors for my transient colleagues. It was a beautiful example of how the navy is a true family and so willing to be there for one another in a time of need.

Muster was held at 5 AM Saturday morning. There were about two hundred of us now that we had been joined with those assigned to the Second FSSG from Naval Hospital, Camp Lejeune. Once we were assembled, the chaplain offered prayers, and families began the arduous and very sad process of saying good-bye to loved ones. It was heartbreaking to watch the young children cling to their fathers and mothers as they bid their final farewells.

Prior to leaving for Cherry Point, North Carolina, we made one final stop at the armory, where we picked up our pistols and ammunition. I stepped up to the barred window, showed my military identification card and pistol data card, and became the sole proprietor of this weapon that would serve as my "last resort" life-saving device. As the supply petty officer handed me this weapon, he said, "God speed, Commander," and I knew he meant it. His words touched my heart, and I thanked him.

From Camp Lejeune, we traveled by bus to Marine Corps Air Station, Cherry Point. This last stateside base served as the place where all our gear would be thoroughly processed for clearance. We were allowed just one seabag and one carry-on bag. A strict weight limit had been mandated for each seabag, and should the bag exceed that specified amount, items would be indiscriminately discarded. Because we would be flying into Kuwait, a territory that could easily come under fire, we had to carry our gas masks, helmets, and weapons on our person, along with our carry-on bag. Fortunately, I had packed my carry-on with only the barest of essentials—a washcloth, a clean pair of underwear, a clean T-shirt, tampons, a toothbrush, jellybeans, and a few energy bars.

Once cleared for transport, we were sent to a hangar-bay area that consisted of nothing more than a large enclosed shell with a very cold cement floor. We made ourselves as comfortable as possible because this waiting period would drag on for several hours. Periodically, we would hear news about our plane's status. The news was that the plane was delayed, delayed, and delayed again. We offered support and reassurance to one another as best we could. Sitting on the cold cement floor, knowing that we were headed into a world none of us had ever experienced before, we began to form personal bonds with one another.

Food provided us with some semblance of comfort, and we sustained ourselves by eating donuts, potato chips, and energy bars. At this point, though, I realized I needed to practice self-discipline and conserve my meager supply of energy bars. We were on the verge of entering a chaotic and unpredictable world where confusion and chaos would reign. I knew nothing could be taken for granted, and I had no idea when I might have access to food again. Other than the potential of having no food, I had no idea what else I would be facing.

Finally, our transport, a United Airlines carrier, arrived. Gear and seabags were quickly loaded, and we boarded the plane shortly after midnight. My day had started at 3 AM, and I was exhausted after not having the opportunity to sleep for twenty-two hours.

The captains and commanders were seated in the plane's first-class section. Unlike my experience with the cramped seating spaces of the Bluebird school bus, I found ample room to stretch out and relax. It was true bliss! The all-volunteer crew on this United Airlines flight was phenomenal. No matter what was asked for, whether it was a bottle of water or information specific to flight time, each member was there for us and enthusiastically met our every need.

The plane was filled with signs and symbols of American patriotism, loyalty, and support for those of us who were headed into the unknown world of war. A large American flag was proudly displayed directly in front of me, and smaller American flags were displayed everywhere throughout the plane's cabin. The flight crew, consisting of more mature folks who had transported troops to the Persian Gulf in 1991 during Desert Storm and to other hostile locations throughout the world, proudly wore red, white, and blue uniforms as a show of support for us and what we were about to do. They were well aware that they were putting their own lives in danger, yet they had volunteered to be with us, to provide extraordinary service to us, and to do all in their power to ensure that we were as comfortable as possible as we flew to Kuwait. I could readily feel their sense of pride, support, concern, and caring for every single one of us on that flight, and it gave me chills. It also provided me with a gentle, calming sense of comfort, and I was finally able to sleep.

The first eight hours of our flight ended in a refueling stop in Germany around 2 AM eastern standard time (EST). As many of my colleagues raced for the phones to call their loved ones to offer words of reassurance and, perhaps, to say good-bye again, I decided that I really did not want to awaken my family. I had already said my good-byes, and they knew how much I loved them. All I really wanted to do was to wash my face, brush my teeth, and freshen up as much as possible using supplies I had carried in my carry-on bag.

The Red Cross had set up a few tables that offered some basic grooming supplies, hot coffee, and cookies. The volunteers working at these tables were gracious, supportive, and extremely generous in assisting us to achieve a sense of comfort while we waited. Once again we could readily see and feel the tremendous support Americans had for us, even those Americans who were thousands of miles from their own homes.

Our wait in Germany was longer than expected because it was not until we had landed that the airline was informed they would not be allowed to refuel in Kuwait. As a result, the crew was directed to land in Kuwait, unload us as quickly as possible, and immediately take off for an alternate destination at which to refuel. It took several hours for the alternate refueling site to be identified and for landing clearance to be granted. Eventually, Turkey was determined to be the place the plane would refuel after the crew unloaded us in Kuwait.

The flight from Germany to Kuwait took another six hours. On our approach to the airfield, the plane's window covers had to be down and all lights turned off. A single flicker of light might alert hostile troops on the ground of our landing, and then the plane could easily serve as a prime target for our enemies. In early to mid-February 2003, Kuwait was not a secure area, and being one of the first military groups to arrive in support of Operation Iraqi Freedom, we were entering into a volatile and hostile region where just about anything could happen.

We landed in Kuwait safely and without incident. Once on the ground, we quickly disembarked. We were like little ants, descending the steps from the plane and being counted one by one. We then passed through two security checkpoints that consisted of two mini-vans equipped with high-tech computers and scanners. Our military ID cards were scanned, and we were asked such questions as "What is

your date of birth?" It was pitch dark, and I know the security personnel could not clearly see us even with their flashlights. Still, expediency
and safety were the main priorities, and the whole process took no
more than twenty seconds. They clearly did not want us to be out in
this potentially volatile and lethal area for any extended period of time,
for we were on the brink of a major military conflict, and we all realized that anything could happen anytime. Our lives were in danger,
and everyone was on high alert, needing to tread softly and, more
important, quickly.

The Kuwaiti buses were waiting at the airstrip to transport us to
our next destination. We had no idea where we were going, and we
did not have much time to really think about it. We just continued to
file along swiftly in our "ant lines," boarding the buses, claiming whatever seat was available, and simply traveling to wherever the bus would
take us.

We had not traveled far before the buses stopped, however. We
then filed off into some sort of staging area surrounded by bunkers,
barbed-wire fences, and trucks sporting machine guns. Although we
were in the middle of the desert somewhere, this place was covered
with rocks, and it was freezing cold. For four and one-half hours we
stood in this dark, cold, wasted, and desolate place, doing nothing
more than waiting and trying to keep warm. To this day, I have no idea
where we were or why we were there, questions I would find myself
pondering frequently as my journey continued.

As the sun started to rise around seven or eight o'clock, we once
again boarded the buses, and I found myself crammed in the back of
the bus with several people. I was totally exhausted and fell asleep for
the bumpy ride, only to awaken two hours later to see nothing but
desert. My last glimpse out the window before falling asleep had been
of the machine-gun trucks that were serving as our escorts. When I
awoke, I tried to look out the window again, but all I could see was
dust. Dust and sand seemed to be coating everything. Then I realized
that what I was seeing was not just dust and sand on the windows, but
instead the vast desert landscape into which we had entered. There was
no distinction between ground and horizon. Everything as far as I

could see had become nothing more than brown sand. I remember thinking "I am in hell now. This has got to be hell."

The road we were driving on consisted of the same brown sand that was creating this personal hell. Everything looked the same—just sand, sand, and more sand as far as the eye could see. The world into which we had entered was flat, dull, and ugly, broken up only by a fleeting glimpse of a wild dog or a small sage shrub. The sight of this enormous and seemingly infinite brown gritty sand landscape was not only dreary and oppressive but also very eerie. How our bus drivers knew where they were going and how we arrived at our next destination remain mysteries to me. Still, eventually, the buses would stop, and we would enter a world and a lifestyle few, if any, of us had ever experienced before.

# 6

# OUR NEW HOME

The buses finally stopped at a place called Camp Guadalcanal, a small site within a larger American-controlled area designated and named Camp Coyote. Our new "home," one of several small encampments in this northern vicinity of Kuwait just south of the Kuwait-Iraq border, consisted of a dug-out sandbox surrounded by a sand wall berm approximately eight to ten feet in height. Concertina wire, sandbags, and a guard shed staffed by marine guards protected the entrance to the camp. Home was nothing more than several old canvas tents and a lot of sand. We had no phone, no pizza, no Taco Bell, no e-mail. We were told some camps and bases somewhere in Kuwait had these conveniences, but ours was definitely not one of them. Our modern conveniences included gravel that had been spread on the ground within this sand-walled complex to diminish the ever-present sand from invading our noses, mouths, and other bodily orifices. We also had electricity, with a few lightbulbs strung within the interior of our tents. To us, simply having electricity was a true luxury.

Two tents had been designated for female berthing. My assigned tent was packed with more than twenty female officers from the Portsmouth and Camp Lejeune contingents, as well as others from Jacksonville, Florida. After collecting our seabags from the buses, we began to set up our gear within the tents, which featured a plank wood floor, dim lighting, canvas walls, and a canvas roof. We claimed our small living and berthing spaces, and I chose one near the tent's opening so I could see outside and feel more in control of my environment. Later we would string rope up so we would have a place to dry our clothes.

Adaptation to basic wartime survival began immediately. Because we were located a mere twenty-three miles from the border with Iraq, we were required to wear our Kevlar vests and helmets and to carry our gas masks and pistols with us at all times, except when we were taking showers or participating in physical-readiness training. And even though we were not actually required to wear this gear during those activities, we had to have it readily accessible, either just outside the shower door or strapped to our waists.

Feeling cramped, uncomfortable, and vulnerable, and living within the small, confined, and uncivilized space of our berthing tents, we did not always get along with one another. The squabbles we had were often silly, consisting of such unimportant, mundane things as who was first at a particular spot and who would bunk next to whom. Feeling lost and having little control over this bleak, empty environment, we tried to take reign over simple things that we believed would give us an increased sense of comfort and stability. We soon realized that stability and even comfort were concepts sacrificed when we boarded the plane in North Carolina. Our American way of life, with all the luxury and comfort to which we were accustomed, had been replaced with nothing more than the basic essentials of survival, namely, shelter, food, water, and clean air. Even these small things would not always be readily available to us.

My bed consisted of my sleeping bag and a mat placed on the plywood floor. Chairs were constructed from boxes and reinforced by empty water-bottle containers that served as supports so the box would not be crushed by our body weight. We secured ropes to our box chairs and carried them with us wherever we went, including meals, classes, and informal gatherings.

A highly valued commodity, our box chairs were built over the course of several days. We were each issued one meal ready to eat (MRE) and two one-and-one-half-liter bottles of water daily. Construction of a sturdy chair required at least six empty water bottles, and we were always on the prowl for an opportunity to acquire "an empty." Being able to sit on something, anything, other than the hard wooden floor was a luxury.

Shower facilities had been constructed and were designated male and female. We were allowed to take a three-minute shower every other day when we had an adequate water supply. Some members of our group arbitrarily broke the rules and would shower every day, diminishing the water supply and breaking down morale. "Job johnnies," or little outhouses, maintained by local civilians, were also set up along the berm. These primitive structures provided little more than a means for us to take care of our basic needs in some semblance of privacy.

Our mess tent provided morning and evening meals prepared and supplied by Kuwaiti civilians. Breakfast consisted of green eggs, bread, cold coffee, and—rarely—fruit. I refused to eat the green eggs and sustained myself by eating two pieces of bread and a cup of cold coffee each morning. Our evening meal usually consisted of one meat dish, such as chicken, fish, or lamb, and sides of rice or potatoes.

The dining facility had no tables or chairs, so we relied heavily on our water-bottle box chairs for some semblance of comfort and civility. The Kuwaitis would bring in the boxes of hot food and set them on tables made of scrap wood. We would line up, collect our ration of food, and, carrying both our food and our box chairs, find a place to plant ourselves. Then we would sit, eat, talk, and simply look forward to returning to our tents to sleep.

Nights in this newfound hell were bitter cold, the temperature dipping well below 40 degrees. Having been diagnosed with Raynaud's disease several years earlier, I was extremely sensitive to the cold, and my prescribed medication to prevent my peripheral arteries from vasoconstriction did little to provide me comfort. The cold nights, combined with sleeping on the wood floor in a sleeping bag, were a miserable experience. I tried desperately to achieve some semblance of warmth, but even when I wore two pairs of socks and three layers of clothes to sleep in, the cold always seemed to find its way into my sleeping bag.

A brief nightly hike to the john was a gloomy adventure. Dressed in our sleeping bags, we would find another "battle buddy" with the same nightly need (we were never to venture outside our tents at night alone), join forces, and somehow manage to find our way to and from the johnnies, guided by nothing more than the dim glow of a red-lens flashlight. Finding someone in the middle of the night with the same urgency to urinate became a major challenge. No one wanted to leave the relative warmth of the tent to wander outside, protected from the cold by little more than a sleeping bag. I quickly learned to consume fewer fluids than what we were allocated on a daily basis in order to avoid dealing with this unpleasant nocturnal excursion.

It did not take long before a relatively "typical" daily routine was established. I would crawl out of my sleeping bag at 5:30 AM. Carrying my toothbrush, toothpaste, and gas mask, I would find a buddy, and we would head for one of the johns. It would be pitch dark, and our route would be illuminated by nothing more than the red flashlight I wore on my head. Returning to the tent, I would change my clothes, grab my gear, and head to our 6 AM muster. I soon acquired the skill of strategically placing my essentials around my small berthing space so I could dress quickly. I thought I had completely mastered this blind skill of dressing efficiently and expediently in the dark until the day came when I mistakenly donned the underwear of one of my tent mates. We all had a good laugh over that one.

During morning muster, our pistols, magazines, and bullets were inspected to ensure that all items were accounted for. The Plan of the Day was read, and we were informed of various lectures that would be offered from 9 AM until 11 AM, as well as any other special events taking place that day. We were also issued our daily ration of two water bottles and an MRE.

Once dismissed from muster, we headed to the mess tent, where I would consume my meager morning ration of bread and cold coffee. I was adamant in my resolve not to eat those nasty green eggs! Following breakfast, I would meet with the anesthesia providers from the Bravo and Charlie companies, and we would review a variety of anesthesia-specific topics, such as rigging portable handheld ventilators and setting up portable oxygen generators. We would also discuss potential-case scenarios as well as such supply-and-demand issues as providing blood transfusions during mass trauma. Then we would go to the training tent to attend one of the lectures that provided us with detailed information specific to caring for a variety of battle injuries, including thoracic, pelvic, neck, orthopedic, abdominal, and so on. The lectures were excellent, and we acquired critical information in preparation for caring for the wounded, as well as essential survival training that would keep us alive.

Despite the instability of this world, I always made time for physical exercise. Following the morning lecture, and weather permitting, I would run several times around the three-quarter-mile perimeter of our camp. Running while carrying my gas mask was tricky but doable. On the days when fierce winds made running impossible, I would walk the perimeter for a total distance of three miles in full gear or do sit-ups and push-ups in my tent.

Washing our bodies and clothes became a challenge as our water supply quickly began to diminish. After being in camp for a week, we did not have ample water for our three-minute rinse-off shower, so I would use my two bottles of drinking water or some premoistened towelettes to try to wash the sand and dirt from my hair and body. We hand washed all of our clothes as best we could with non-potable water and hung them to dry on the ropes we had strung up inside our tents. Nothing was ever really clean: not our bodies, our clothes, or our belongings.

At noon we took our MREs over to the chow tent where we ate, socialized, and shared stories of home with one another. Then we would return for more classes until the 4 PM muster where, once again, our pistols, magazines, and bullet counts were reported and verified and new information was passed.

We spent our evenings completing domestic chores such as brushing out the sand from our sleeping bags and off our gear. It was amazing how the sand would get into everything and be everywhere. I used this time to take apart my pistol, thoroughly cleaning it and all the bullets inside the two magazines.

My favorite time of day was our evening mealtime, for it signaled to me that I had but a few more hours before I would have a chance to daydream about home as I fell off to sleep. Daydreaming of home provided comfort and reassured me that this dismal world was only temporary. Each night as I headed back to my tent, I would find myself being thankful for another day without war and so appreciative of the smallest things in life.

Small things were critical to us. What we had once taken for granted at our homes stateside became a very big deal for those of us in this barren, miserable, desert environment. One evening as I was returning from the chow tent, I saw six to eight of my shipmates searching with their red-filtered flashlights for something on the ground. It reminded me of how people would stop, gather round, and search for someone's lost contact lens. I knew it would be impossible to locate a lost contact lens in the dark among all the sand and gravel, guided only by very dim red-tinted lighting.

Not until I approached this group did I understand that the search was not for a contact lens; instead, they were looking for the cap of a Chapstick tube. I immediately joined the search, as did several others. Petroleum jelly lip balm was important to us, and the loss of the tube's cap was a very big deal. Without the cap, dirt and sand would quickly cover the end of the tube, causing it to solidify and become useless. No one wanted to see that happen, especially when the sand and dirt of our surroundings were coating and destroying everything else we owned. Eventually, and fortunately, we were able to find the cap. For me, this was just one more example that nothing could be taken for granted and that we were a long, long way from the normalcy of our homes in the United States.

Receiving mail from home was a pure joy. I was blessed with a very supportive family and many friends who wrote letters and sent packages. Some letters were from those friends I had grown to know over the years, and others were from new friends I had never met. My sister had informed those with whom she worked at the Blue Ball National Bank in Blue Ball, Pennsylvania, that I was in Kuwait, preparing to move into Iraq with the marines. I began to receive letters from her coworkers and friends and then from her friends' friends. I received mail from churches, card groups, and bingo groups. The support was overwhelming, and I cherished every letter, for each one provided me with a constant reminder of how appreciative those back home were of the sacrifice we were making in our effort to safeguard our homeland.

Mail delivery was hit or miss, totally dependent on the supply trucks' ability to safely traverse the desert from Kuwait City. At times, weeks would pass without mail, and then suddenly, seemingly out of nowhere, we would be pleasantly surprised with the receipt of numerous letters and packages. We never knew when or if we would receive mail; we only hoped we would. I felt sad for those who did not receive a package or a letter from home. Those of us fortunate to receive letters and packages readily shared our American treasures with those who received nothing.

Occasionally, we would have movie night. One laptop computer with PowerPoint presentation capabilities was routinely used during our daytime training sessions. This unit was made available to us for recreational use during the evening. A corpsman had brought several DVDs with him, which he readily shared. These movies provided a few hours of diversion, and for those brief moments, I would feel like I was back in the United States. To make this experience even more representative of home, we would save our Lifesavers or Skittle candies from our MRE packets just so we could munch on them while viewing the films. We may not have had popcorn, but we did everything we could to develop our own special comfort zone that resembled some visage of normal American life.

Prior to showing whatever movie was to be the "feature of the day," the person presenting the movie would project a short film that depicted various landmarks and symbols of the United States accompanied by Lee Greenwood's musical rendition of "Proud to Be an American." No matter how often this film was played or how many times we watched it, it always brought tears to our eyes and validated why we were where we were. It would ignite the love and passion we felt for the United States, the American way of life, and our fellow citizens. It gave us a sense of purpose and true meaning for what we were enduring and what we would be called to do in the future.

Gas mask drills occurred frequently, both during daylight hours and at night. We had no way of knowing whether they were simple drills or the real thing. We took no chances and responded immediately when the alarm sounded. Donning our masks, we ensured that we created a tight seal not only on our own masks but also on those of our battle buddies. We became so proficient at donning the masks that we could accomplish this task in less than nine seconds. We would continue to wear them for thirty to sixty minutes before receiving word that all was clear.

The weather was totally unpredictable. Sandstorms were inevitable and a constant worry. We were in the middle of the desert, surrounded by nothing more than sand, with little to no protection. We were at the mercy of Mother Nature, and she did not always look on us with favor. Winds were fierce and, as I would soon learn, very capable of creating and instilling total devastation and chaos into our brittle, makeshift desert world.

# 7

# GEARING UP FOR WAR

On Sunday, 23 February, we were called for a briefing to be given by Lt. Gen. James T. Conway, U.S. Marine Corps, commanding general of the 1st MEF. General Conway was scheduled to address all the combat marines and those who were there to support them.

Those assigned to Camp Guadalcanal and others residing in area camps were bused over to a desolate, exposed area in the middle of the desert, where we stood for several hours waiting for the entire group of approximately six thousand to assemble. On the horizon we saw several platoons of U.S Marines marching in ranks, proudly displaying the American flag. Whereas we had the luxury of being bused to this remote area, these fearless combat marines had marched in formation for miles to hear the general speak.

When General Conway arrived, we were in formation within our designated companies and camps, standing at attention and eagerly waiting to be informed of our destiny. Observing that we were in mixed ranks, the general ordered us to relocate to a different designated area, for he wanted to address the officers separately from the enlisted troops.

More time passed as we reassembled. Finally, General Conway spoke to us about why we were going north, emphasizing that the date, time, and exact place were still unknown. Sensing our apprehension, he told us that fear was a natural feeling, one to be addressed and then let go. He stressed the need to kill the enemy, for in killing the enemy, we would be saving ourselves and our shipmates.

The enemy could be anyone, he explained, man, woman, or child, and they would be counting on our American sensibilities of civility and compassion. As Americans, we were naturally vulnerable, willing to offer a helping hand when we perceived a need. As a result, we could easily be seduced by the enemy in the form of children or women holding children who might approach our convoys asking for help. Instinctively viewing them as harmless and in need, we might let down our guard and extend a helping hand. By doing so, we could easily place our lives and the lives of our buddies in great danger, for these harmless-appearing individuals might be carrying bombs and explosives designed to destroy us. We were told, in no uncertain terms, to kill anyone who approached our convoy.

General Conway was a warrior. His goal was to push north into Iraq, kill the people who needed to be killed, get to Baghdad, and annihilate the brutality, savagery, and global threat inherent in Saddam Hussein's dictatorship. This was to be done quickly and efficiently, with minimal loss of life to our American troops. His message was simple: be on your guard at all times and do not hesitate to kill. The enemy could and would take all forms, and we needed to be ready with a steadfast resolve to kill any Iraqi who approached us.

I could not help but wonder, as I did before we arrived here, whether I would be able to fire my pistol and destroy the life of another human being. Killing was a concept that was totally foreign to me and against my nature, both professionally and personally. I thought about my life and the lives of my battle buddies and how any of us could easily become one of the wounded or a fatality. Instead of pursuing our mission to provide life-saving medical and surgical care to others, we might also be recipients of this care. We were very much in harm's way, and this reality ignited feelings and emotions that were so foreign and so painful to me that I simply could not ponder them for long. Instead, I comforted myself with the belief that I would do the right thing when and if I was faced with the awesome, gut-wrenching, and devastating decision to kill another.

Following the briefing, we returned to our life at Camp Guadalcanal, with General Conway's comments resonating in our heads and in our hearts. Tension within the camp was almost palpable. We had time to reflect on the general's words and to discuss not only what the months ahead would bring but also how we might react to this unknown, almost unimaginable, future. It stimulated feelings of anger, caution, and uncertainty as to whether we could and would make the right decision at the right time.

That night a gas mask drill was called. When an American drone flew over our area on its way to Iraq, we were reminded that the enemy was watching our every move just as we were watching its.

Few of us were able to sleep that night, tossing and turning in our sleeping bags, haunted by the words of General Conway and thinking about what lay ahead. Although we knew our lives were at risk, this was not our primary concern, for we had deployed willingly to Kuwait and Iraq aware of the danger and harm that could easily be inflicted on us. The source of our restless sleep was the unwanted codicil that was now added to our primary medical support mission.

Our mission, to save the lives of our soldiers, sailors, aircrews, and any and all other war casualties, might require us to destroy lives in order to save lives. It was a simple, rational concept in the face of war and perhaps easily comprehensible for those veterans who had fought valiantly on the battlefields of the past. For those of us who had spent our entire lives mastering the art of healing and caring for others no matter what it entailed, taking the life of another human being was inconceivable. We would need many days and sleepless nights to comprehend this fully. Would it be truly possible to perform patient care with an Ambu bag (a self-inflating bag used to help a patient breathe during resuscitation) in one hand and a pistol in the other?

Making preparations to move north into combat was both an individual and a group labor. I spent hours loading my Alice pack and sorting my gear and personal items so they would fit into one seabag. We had no guarantee that the one allotted seabag would follow us or be delivered to us at our next camp, so the contents of the Alice pack became critical to our survival. It needed to contain all items we believed we would need to live on for approximately three to five days. Making decisions about what to pack in this small knapsack would be an ongoing, painstaking process.

Because we believed we would be at war within a week, our daily training sessions and briefings became more intense and earnest as the days passed. Training sessions emphasized our need to provide advanced trauma life-support measures to the best of our abilities. Our role would be one of damage control: maintaining airway and vital signs, stopping any bleeding, irrigating and packing wounds, and getting the patient transferred as soon as possible.

Our four original companies were consolidated into three companies known as Alpha, Bravo, and Charlie. This realignment was completed for several reasons: there was not enough logistical support, such as vehicles and generators, to move and sustain four companies; some equipment and essential gear that had been shipped was either broken or missing; more Forward Resuscitation Surgical System (FRSS) teams and Shock Trauma Platoons (STPs) were being formed and required personnel; and an additional ten-cot-housing holding company also needed personnel. Fortunately, I continued to remain a member of the Bravo Surgical Company.

Bravo Company had a sixty-bed patient capacity. Twenty of these beds were dedicated to intensive care and surgical recovery. Our company, approximately two hundred personnel, was further divided into platoons: a triage (initial receiving and evaluation area)/evacuation platoon, a surgical platoon, and a holding platoon. My surgical platoon was made up of three operating rooms (ORs), with two operating tables per room. We had six surgeons: two general, one orthopedic, two obstetrics/gynecology (OB/GYN), and one podiatrist. I found it interesting and rather strange that the OB/GYN surgeons and the podiatrist were assigned to a frontline surgical company. Still, my years in the Navy Nurse Corps had taught me that even though some of us had been designated "specialists" in one field, we were also very much "generalists." We had the ability to adapt quickly and to serve in roles not necessarily prescribed or totally focused on one particular medical/surgical specialty. We possessed many general medical-surgical skills, were highly versatile, and would competently fill whatever need or demand was required to save the lives of our American troops. The skill of the OB/GYN doctors was converted to serving as first assistants to the general surgeons. They would suture wounds and incisions so the general surgeons could start another procedure.

The experience and clinical skills of the nurses assigned to Bravo Surgical Company varied. We had two experienced intensive care nurses and several young nurses with less than a year of service in the navy. Six of the nurses had experience exclusively in labor and delivery, and several of the lieutenants had been working in clinics prior to being deployed. The few senior nurses in our ranks had not been involved in direct patient care for several years.

As an echelon-two surgical company, we, along with the FRSS teams, would receive casualties immediately after they received basic first aid from echelon-one personnel on the field. Once stabilized at our level, the wounded would be transported to an echelon-three facility, an amphibious ship or a hospital ship, and eventually taken for definitive care at a land-based hospital. The medical administrators assigned to our camp would schedule where the patients were to be taken. Their exact final destination would remain unknown to me.

Our war training continued, and the level of tension within the camp escalated. I prayed every day that I would make the right decision in caring for the wounded, for I steadfastly believed these brave warriors deserved that and more. I thought about the possibility of my own life being destroyed, but my greatest fear was that I might not know enough to help keep some sailor or marine alive. We all shared this fear, and we took our training sessions very seriously.

In addition to the general training sessions offered throughout the day, the anesthesia staffs of both the Bravo and Charlie companies would meet daily to discuss concerns and to review case scenarios. We called ourselves the "Kuwait/United Navy Anesthesia Society." We were a highly spirited, knowledgeable, and cohesive group, determined to share any and all information that might help save the lives of those in our care.

More and more gear and equipment arrived each day. Plastic-backed chairs for the chow hall/mess tent were delivered, and I was finally issued a cot on which to sleep. I greatly appreciated these improved accommodations, but, more important, I was pleased that our OR and anesthesia equipment had also arrived. Discussions during the daily sessions of our newly formed Kuwait/United Navy Anesthesia Society were spent sharing information about the OR setup and exploring ideas and options for acquiring extra electrocardiogram cables, oxygen tanks, and various perishable items that would help us save lives. We found ourselves hoarding supplies of all kinds and living like scavengers.

We had an opportunity to erect our surgical tent, an arduous task that took about an hour to complete. Unlike the tents used by the fleet hospital units, our tent had no air-conditioning or heating system. This simple structure featured little more than a sand floor and minimal lighting. We spent hours arranging and rearranging surgical and anesthesia equipment so that this rustic "surgical suite" would be efficient, functional, and a lifesaver for those who were entrusted to our care. We even positioned the OR tables so they were head to head, allowing one anesthesia provider to administer anesthesia to two patients simultaneously.

We could accommodate only about sixty patients with our supply of such perishable items as surgical sponges, needles, syringes, and endotracheal tubes. We knew we would need to recycle these items to the best of our ability to have the necessary supplies available for all the wounded we anticipated. The blood from surgical sponges would be squeezed out so the sponge could be reused on the same patient. Needles to withdraw medications from ampules and vials, syringes, endotracheal tubes, and the breathing circuit for our anesthesia machines would be rinsed with 5 percent hypochlorite bleach (diluted) and reused. We hoped these measures would ensure that we had the supplies we needed to provide lifesaving care to our wounded troops.

We also tried to come to grips with our obligations under the Geneva Convention. According to that agreement, we were obligated to render care to all enemy prisoners of war (EPWs). Because we were limited in supplies, personnel, and general facilities, the prospect of this obligation became a real and difficult ethical issue. I prayed every day that I would find the strength to make the best decision and to do what was right.

# 8

# A BATTLE WITH
# MOTHER NATURE

Although we continued to focus our efforts primarily on preparing ourselves mentally, physically, and emotionally to move north into enemy territory, we also kept a vigilant eye on the weather. I had never been anywhere in my life where the weather was so unpredictable, extreme, and relentless. It was not unusual to experience a 20- to 30-degree drop in temperature in less than an hour, or for the winds to be calm one moment and racing at forty miles per hour thirty minutes later. Dense fog frequently shrouded our camp in the early morning hours, and heavy rain showers would occur with little warning. One time we even experienced a hailstorm.

On 6 March, the day began with cloudy skies and frequent downpours of rain. The wind slowly increased throughout the day but did not deter us from our routine of musters and training sessions and the general activities of daily living. We had been informed that our Kuwaiti food providers had brought ice cream as a special treat for our evening meal. Hearing this exciting and enticing news, most of the camp personnel made a mad dash to the chow line, for this was one treat few of us had savored in several weeks, and we doubted we would have the chance again for many months to come.

Departing the chow tent at 6:30 PM, we all noticed that it was unusually dark and the wind speed had increased significantly. As we tried to walk back from the mess tent, the wind was blowing so hard we could not hold our heads upright. We swallowed and breathed in large quantities of dry, brown grit with every step, and the sand felt like glass as it battered our skin and clothing. Although we had flashlights and were wearing goggles, we could not see a thing. We were totally blind and managed to find our way to our berthing tents only by counting the number of tents we passed between the mess tent and the berthing tent we called home.

The wind was soon blowing at a sustained rate well over fifty miles per hour. We could hear the sounds of canvas ripping as the wind pummeled our tents. We immediately declared war on these elements that seemed determined to destroy the meager home and all semblance of comfort we had created in this dismal and godforsaken land. Our battle with Mother Nature had begun.

The center poles supporting the roof of our berthing tent began to disengage from their holders, and the top and side seams began to separate. The electric wires and lightbulbs swayed violently. We all ran for a section of the tent to hold, pull, or anchor. We grabbed flaps, siding, poles, and ropes and blindly fought this battle of survival. This was our home, and we would not let it be destroyed without a fierce fight.

We fought for hours, some holding flashlights in an attempt to illuminate our efforts while others pulled, tugged, and even tried to sew the seams closed by threading cord through the canvas. We were fierce warriors, steadfast in our resolve to save this home of ours. Some were inside the tent's enclosure, propping up poles and fixtures, while others were outside pounding stakes and tightening ropes and tethers.

Unfortunately, Mother Nature proved to be a tenacious and unrelenting opponent. The winds continued to wreak havoc on our humble abode, and as the tent's seams split further apart and the frame began to collapse, safety became the main issue. We needed to get out, let go, and move away. Several of our battle buddies nearby came to help us retrieve whatever basic essentials we could locate inside this collapsing structure. We hurriedly grabbed items, threw them into a sack, and ran from beneath the toppling canvas roof just in time to witness our home crumble to the ground. This simple, modest oasis we had created, where we could relax, dream, and find some scant measure of comfort, had become nothing more than a heap of canvas in the sand. We all felt tired, frustrated, and angry. We had lost the battle.

During the course of that eventful and memorable night, the camp lost two primary berthing tents to the daunting and brutal winds of this merciless desert land. Both the junior enlisted male tent and our female officers' tent were demolished.

Carrying my sleeping bag and a small bag of rescued personal items, I left the battlefield and went in search of an alternate berthing space. I felt defeated and extremely tired, and my muscles ached from the battle we had so diligently fought. I was filthy, with every inch of my body covered in sweat and caked with sand. Personal hygiene was not a concern, however. All I wanted and needed was a place, any place, to lie down and rest.

Eventually, I located a spot to spread my sleeping bag within the senior male officers' tent. Some of us had made our way to this dwelling, while others sought refuge in the female enlisted tent. The male occupants of our new temporary home graciously accommodated us even though doing so meant we would all be packed in like sardines. We were disrupting their world and whatever little comfort they had been able to achieve. Still, they welcomed us, and we were grateful. Respect and consideration for our gender differences and need for privacy was not a big issue. It was really a simple matter; when we females needed a private moment, the men simply turned their heads, and we, in turn, provided them with the same act of respect and courtesy.

The wind continued to whip violently throughout the night, and few of us were able to sleep. We frequently needed to venture outside our canvas shelters to retighten ropes, hammer stakes, and move sandbags in an attempt to keep the tent in which we had sought refuge from collapsing. During the brief moments I was able to lie down, I wondered what the morning would bring, how much damage had occurred, and what, if any, of our personal gear we would be able to find.

I felt very vulnerable and small that night. Just as I had started to feel more confident, strong, and ready to move forward into the bloody battlefield of a human war, Mother Nature suddenly came along and slammed me back into reality. Our battle against the elements had reminded me that although we were prepared and could plan, predict, and to some extent even control our future engagements with our human enemies, we had little power over Mother Nature. Her force, timing, and temperament were totally unpredictable, and she had proved herself to be a formidable opponent. That night she was the true victor of a fierce, mighty battle, and I felt humbled.

By morning, the winds had subsided to approximately fifteen miles per hour. During muster, a head count revealed we were all safe and accounted for, and we were provided an opportunity to share our feelings of fear, anger, and loss. We needed to find the positive in what had become a negative situation, something we would struggle to do many more times in the weeks and months ahead.

Despite the havoc we had endured at the hand of Mother Nature, the positive aspects of this seemingly catastrophic event began to surface. Had this vicious storm started in the middle of the night while we were sleeping, many of us might have become trapped beneath the frames and canvas of our tents, possibly sustaining serious injuries from falling poles and light fixtures. We could also have lost more structures than just the two berthing tents. We could have lost everything, leaving us exposed and totally unprotected in this relentless environment. Our periodic moments of grief over our loss were replaced by feelings of thankfulness, and we even started to believe that we had been blessed because not everything had been destroyed. We had saved a few items and would salvage some more; the most important thing was that we were all safe. We also had shelter, and I knew I would be assigned another berthing space that I would once again call home. Our tent may have been destroyed, but our sense of hope and our drive to move forward were very much intact.

In the light of day, we found it hard to believe that the heap of torn canvas and broken poles lying on the ground in a filthy mixture of gravel and dirt had once been a place in which we lived. Seeing it in such a shattered state and remembering the quiet comfort it had provided us was a heartbreaking experience. Despite the tragic sight it posed for us, however, we knew we had no time for tears. We had work to do and could ill afford wasting time or energy wallowing in self-pity.

We joined forces and worked together with one single-minded mission: to recover anything that would assist us in rebuilding our lives. We crawled underneath the dark, suffocating, heavy canvas and gathered and salvaged everything we could find. The task was backbreaking and dirty. We guided and supported one another in an effort to extract our most cherished and essential possessions from the bowels of this heap of rubble. Whatever trivial and petty disagreements we may have had with one another in the past were set aside. We worked together as a team, refusing to give up, and we became more positive as we set about accomplishing this task.

We successfully retrieved all of our war and survival gear and most of our personal items. This achievement was the morale booster we needed. Although we had lost this one lone battle with Mother Nature, we definitely had not lost the war! In many ways we felt invigorated, not only because we survived the battle but also because we had become stronger, more focused, and more confident in our own abilities and those of each other. We had moved beyond simply being individual survivors that day; we had become a team of warriors with an unflinching resolve to fight and destroy the enemy in whatever form it might present itself.

A comprehensive inspection of all the camp's facilities revealed additional damage to our desert canvas world. Several tents had sustained split seams, gaping holes, dislodged stakes, broken rope tethers, and bent framing; debris was strewn everywhere. It would take several days to clean up and repair the damage caused by the windstorm.

Using our small utility knives, we cut canvas from the wreckage of the fallen tents and used the green rope we each carried to sew crude canvas patches together. We sewed seams and patched torn holes. We straightened framing and secured it with additional salvaged rope, stakes, and sandbags. We fixed what we could, and our world began to return to some semblance of normalcy. We again proved to ourselves after several days of hard work that although our ability to work as a team was being tested, we were passing that test with flying colors. It was now time to settle back in and concentrate our efforts once again on preparing for our primary mission—saving the lives of our American troops.

# 9

# SETTLING BACK IN

Because several living quarters had been destroyed or damaged, new berthing accommodations were quickly arranged. My new home was a small tent that was originally designated as Bravo Company's chapel. Too small in which to hold Sunday worship services (both Protestant and Catholic services were held in a much larger tent located in Charlie Company territory), this tent served as a private sanctuary for use by our chaplain, Lt. Laura Bender (also known as "Chaps"), in which to hold spiritual counseling sessions.

The chapel was converted slightly and would now serve double duty as a sanctuary for private counseling sessions during the day and a home for four of us to sleep in during the night. I claimed a corner of this small dwelling, stowed my salvaged gear, including my highly prized box chair, and placed my sleeping bag on the floor. I even took time to rest my aching back, for the strain and turmoil of the previous night had taken its toll on me. I felt every single day of my forty-five years of life.

That first evening in my new home, I sat with my new roommates listening to the comforting sounds of smooth jazz. One of them had brought several music compact disks and a player with her. While the chaplain concentrated on her cross-stitch work, the rest of us read, relaxed, and simply enjoyed a quiet sense of peace that resonated within our souls. It was the most enjoyable evening I had spent in the eighteen days since arriving at Camp Guadalcanal.

We were given one day to rest, recuperate, and reenergize before returning to our rigorous daily schedule. The Protestant worship service held that Sunday, 9 March, featured a sermon titled "Weathering the Storm," a topic we all found to be very appropriate and extremely meaningful, considering our most recent ordeal.

Throughout the next few weeks, our training continued and became even more intense. We spent several days setting up and taking down our surgical hospital tents. It was an exhausting task. The bundled tents were heavy, requiring four to six people to lift and carry them. We all participated in this endeavor, frequently rotating our positions so that each of us knew the precise sequence of tasks from various angles and positions that were required to erect the tents.

We had no assigned stations, division of labor, or assignment of task based on military rank or profession. We simply worked shoulder to shoulder. Although we may have held titles and labels that designated us as enlisted or officer personnel, surgeons, nurses, technicians, and corpsmen, we were simply able-bodied people working together in this endeavor to accomplish a single goal. Egos, status, and military rank were set aside and deemed insignificant. No job was considered too menial, for every task was critical and needed to be performed accurately and precisely in order to raise the tents that would enable us to care for the wounded. We became experts at spreading the canvas, aligning and connecting the framing, fastening ropes, and pounding stakes into the ground. Our proficiency in accomplishing these feats significantly improved with each subsequent practice.

Following the merciless windstorm we had endured, we all held Mother Nature in high regard and knew we needed to be prepared for anything. We practiced setting up the tents in calm weather and in windy conditions, during daylight and at night, and during the cold morning hours and during the smoldering, blistering heat of midday. We were determined to be prepared both for our human enemy and for the wrath of Mother Nature.

Mass-casualty drills, simulating the process of providing care for and moving patients from triage to the OR, the recovery area, the ICU, the postoperative ward, and, finally, the evacuation unit, were held frequently. Each unit would be directed to "put up your tent," and everyone would move into action. After setting up the various tents for the triage area, the ORs, the ICU, and the ward, we would survey our surroundings and discuss the intricacies and basic logistics of our operation. We discussed where supplies would be stored; where to place OR tables, equipment, beds, and lighting; and how to communicate with one another most effectively while the patient was processed through each of these areas. Once everything was in place, we would then walk a mock patient through the system, beginning with that person's arrival in the helicopter or ambulance, through triage, into the OR, and then to the ICU or ward.

We were guided in our efforts by Cdr. Mark Fontana, a general surgeon, who was responsible for making all final medical decisions for the Bravo Surgical Company. After every drill, we would meet as a team to discuss such issues and concerns as limited supplies, wartime criteria for providing blood transfusions, availability of pharmaceutical medications, the need for X-rays, and even the way to handle a death that might occur in one of the various units of our battlefield hospital. We were steadfast in our resolve to provide our wounded with the best care possible, and we tried to prepare for every contingency.

Our morning muster time was changed from 6 AM to 8:15 AM, allowing us additional time to sleep, the weather conditions and the frequency of gas mask drills permitting. During muster, we would receive information and plans about our impending forward movement north, only to discover that the plans would change almost as frequently as the weather. We often joked about these "plans" and considered them to be "etched in Jell-O"—solid and firm one moment, only to become shaky and turning into liquid by the end of the day.

The sounds of heavy artillery fire, combined with the upsurge in the number and frequency of helicopters and jets flying over our area, led us all to believe a declaration of war was very close. Taking these and several other escalated war preparations into account, we began to speculate about the date that war would be declared. My guess was 17 March. Having no access to television or any other news outlet except the scant and erratic information we received during muster, we based our predictions solely on the sights, sounds, and heightened activities surrounding us. We continued to have no definitive idea when we would advance north. All we knew was that we were ready and eager to go.

We were issued diazepam bristojets (individually preset doses of diazepam in syringes for self-injection) to add to our war gear. We were to administer these bristojets to prevent seizures in the event we came into contact with nerve agents. We were also given a month's supply of doxycycline for the prevention of malaria because Iraq's rainy season was just around the corner. A fifteen-day supply of ciprofloxacin hydrochloride, a preventive antidote for anthrax exposure, was also issued.

We began packing our field hospital into International Organization for Standardization (ISO) containers. These massive steel boxes were twenty to forty feet in length and close to nine feet in height. Our entire field hospital, comparable to a stateside medical-surgical trauma center, was to be packed and transported in these durable, enclosed containers. It was extremely hard work that required every morsel of physical strength and fortitude we could muster. A single side of a tent, once rolled, weighed almost two hundred pounds, and the weight of all the equipment and supplies was measured in tons.

The day of 12 March was a long, taxing one because we spent it packing the ISO containers. It was the hottest day we had experienced since our arrival. The heat, combined with the daylong strenuous activity of lifting, pulling, and pushing tons of equipment, tents, and medical supplies into the containers, took its toll on us. By evening, we were all totally exhausted and looking forward to a night of relaxation and sleep.

As nightfall approached, however, the winds increased. Remembering well the devastation we had experienced from the last windstorm, we readily donned our helmets and goggles, exited our home, and began tightening the ropes and securing the stakes that were the only real supports of this small dwelling that housed all of our belongings and provided us with a small measure of safety and comfort. The winds steadily and rapidly increased as we labored, blowing sand into our mouths and lungs and coating every inch of our bodies.

After securing our tent to the greatest extent possible, Chaps and I headed to one of the job johnnies. The wind was blowing so hard that we had to hold onto one another just to remain upright and to keep from losing one another. Our flashlights illuminated nothing but a massive, swirling, thick curtain of sand in front of us. Blindly, we trudged our way through this sand in the direction we thought one of the johnnies was located. Had it not been for the sand wall berm surrounding the camp, we would easily have walked straight out into the open desert. The johnnie was located a mere two feet to the right of where we stood facing the berm, yet we could not see it. We finally located it more by feel than by sight.

As we struggled blindly in an attempt to return home, we found it to be impossible to distinguish one tent from another. Believing I had successfully guided us home, I inadvertently entered the executive officer's tent, which was located next to ours. As I crawled through the tent's hatch, the officer was sitting with his back to me. When he glanced over his shoulder in my direction, all he could see was a goggled, sand-powdered creature crawling slowly toward him. Startled at this unexpected and strange sight, he screamed, causing me to scream. I certainly was not expecting to see him, and he had no idea who I was or whether I was even human. Although it caused us to experience momentary fright that night, we both would share many laughs together during the next few weeks when we would recall this humorous incident.

Once Chaps and I finally did locate our true home, we decided to leave the lower part of the tent's flap door untied and to open the panels on the opposite side of it. This would allow the wind to flow through the tent, diminishing the relentless pounding to its sides and decreasing the strain on the frame and ropes that were holding it upright. We knew the wind, along with the massive amount of sand it contained, would ultimately force the tent to come crashing down on top of us if we did not vent it in this way.

Our sleeping bags became our only real shelter from the sand and grit being violently blown throughout our home. We crawled into them, covering ourselves as best as we could, and settled down to what would be a very tumultuous and sleepless night.

As the night wore on, the wind gradually began to subside. Sometime in the middle of the night, I needed to visit the john again but was not looking forward to another trek outdoors. Still, I disengaged myself from the fragile cover of my sleeping bag; grabbed my mask, goggles, and flashlight; woke a battle buddy; and we headed out.

With less wind and improved visibility, our trip to and from the john was considerably easier, faster, and much less traumatic for the executive officer living next door and for us. It was sometime around 1 AM. Determining the exact time was impossible because sand had caked the face of my wristwatch with such a thick opaque coating that the numbers could not be seen even when the watch was illuminated internally and externally. This, I soon discovered, was just a small example of what we would be facing when our home and its contents were revealed to us in the light of day.

The next day, the wind continued to blow, swirling sand and grit in its unyielding, though somewhat diminished, assault on our camp. Fortunately, all of the tents had survived and remained standing. Wind and sand were a dreaded combination, and it never ceased to amaze us how sand could invade and imbed itself into the deepest, smallest, most remote recesses of our tent's interior. Our belongings were caked with it, and it had even managed to find its way inside sealed plastic bags and containers. Our sleeping bags were full of sand, both inside and out, and all our clothing was filthy.

Cleanup became an act of futility. We could not rid all of our meager yet highly prized and cherished belongings of all the mire and grime in which they were encapsulated. We hand washed our clothes, returning them to a "clean dirty" versus "dirty dirty" state. Weeks of hand washing clothes and never getting them totally clean caused them to appear dingy and gray. Clean dirty referred to clothes that had been recently washed; dirty dirty referred to clothes that needed to be washed. We worked diligently, cleaning what we could, all the while fantasizing about the day we would construct a massive bonfire and readily destroy all that we had brought with us to this desolate land. There was no way we would bring this filth, including our clean dirty clothes, back into our stateside homes.

# 10

## GROWING WEARY

For twenty-five days I had existed and adapted to this ever-changing hellacious sandbox world located somewhere in the bowels of Kuwait. I had no idea of either my precise location (somewhere between twenty-five and thirty-five miles from the Iraqi border) or when and if I would ever depart from it. I had lost my first "home" and survived several merciless sandstorms. I was exhausted from the physical demands required to load the ISO containers, clean the filth from our windblown, sand-filled tent, and function on little to no sleep.

We seemed to be doing nothing other than spinning our wheels, performing repetitive, burdensome tasks, only to be told the following day to undo that which we had carried out. I wanted desperately to move on in pursuit of the mission for which we had been sent, to see something, anything, other than the flat, dull, brown sand on the horizon. I longed to see green grass, my spring bulbs blooming in the garden of my stateside home, and birds flying overhead or perched contentedly on the branches of trees. I also needed to feel worthwhile by providing the patient care for which I was trained. I had grown weary, and my spirits began to falter.

I was not alone in feeling disheartened. We all were beginning to feel the stress and strain inherent in living day after day within this austere environment. We all missed our families and our friends back home, and we believed the sooner the war began, the sooner we would be able to go home and reunite with them. Waiting was miserable, and sitting idle began to gnaw at our positive "can-do" attitudes.

As survivors and, more important, as the warriors we had become, we refused to surrender to this strong, compelling sense of despondency that had invaded our world. Bonding ever closer with one another, we declared all-out war on the negative and defeatist emotions and mental attitudes we had begun to experience. It was time to take action, to take control over our emotional worlds, and to reignite our survivor spirit.

Strategies in this battle for emotional integrity incorporated a variety of tactics, ranging from various social endeavors to lone quiet moments spent in reflection, where we would remind ourselves of what we had instead of what we lacked. We constantly sought out basic, simple pleasures that would boost our fledgling spirits.

We would frequently gather and spend time doing nothing more than cracking bad jokes and sharing tales of our lives back in the States. We watched movies, shared meals together, and celebrated the smallest, most trivial events such as the delivery of fresh water to the camp or the rare meals of spaghetti, fried fish, or hamburgers that were erratically provided. All our efforts became focused toward validating the worth and merit of one another and finding things for which to be grateful. We pursued anything and everything to elevate our spirits and to steer our attitudes on a more positive course.

The receipt of mail, even when it arrived almost a month after it was posted stateside, helped to lift my spirits and the spirits of my battle buddies. There was nothing like reading a letter from home or, better yet, receiving a package filled with Power Bars, premoistened towelettes, dried fruit, Chapstick, and packets of Kool-Aid.

The letters from my friends in the States inquired about the "fast food setup," gymnasium, swimming pool, and phone and e-mail facilities and capabilities within our camp. They were apparently watching CNN coverage that was being broadcast from other camps in Kuwait where these luxuries actually did exist. Our camp was the extreme opposite of what was being projected on their television screens. Fast food was something we could savor only in our dreams, and simply having water was a treat for us. At least we did have water more often than not.

The weather conditions also began to improve. Daylight temperatures now ranged from 75 to 85 degrees, and although the winds continued to blow, they seemed less fierce and destructive. For me, the biggest improvement was the elevated temperature at night. Instead of dipping below 40 degrees, the nighttime temperatures were in the high 50s. I found that I no longer needed to sleep in seven layers, cocooning myself in three layers within my sleeping bag just to achieve some semblance of warmth. I also no longer needed to sleep with the clothes I planned to wear the following day tucked inside the sleeping bag to warm them up—that trick I had learned in Kansas twenty-three long years earlier.

One night in mid-March, Tish, one of the female lieutenants, invited me and several others to come over to her tent for a special "Friday night out." I knew it would not come anywhere close in comparison with a Friday night out on the town back home in the States, but I was very intrigued by the invitation. Dressed in my best dingy, gray-tinged, clean dirty clothes, I walked to Tish's tent and gathered with the others for this special event.

It proved to be a fun evening and perhaps one of my best since arriving in Kuwait. Tish had received a sixty-pound box from home filled with facial products, hand creams, foot lotions, and more. We spent several hours giving each other hand and foot massages, facials, manicures, and pedicures, laughing and giggling all the while as we pursued these frilly endeavors. It was such a "girl thing," and that evening we felt just that—like girls, instead of warriors. The emulsion hand creams and oils we used were literally sucked in when we put them on our severely dried skin. Although the softness these items produced was short lived, it was wonderful to savor this temporary luxury. Our activities that evening were meaningless and silly nonsense, and we loved every minute of it!

We also found release and positive emotions through regular daily exercise regimes. I continued to run my early morning laps around the perimeter of the camp, and several of us would often gather in the afternoon to walk the perimeter again in full gear.

Daily intelligence briefings provided us with information that was reliable, yet also quite frustrating at times. At one point we were informed that six countries of the United Nations Security Council had voted against going to war, wanting instead to extend Saddam Hussein's deadline to turn over his weapons of mass destruction. For those of us sitting in a hellhole a mere thirty-five miles or less from the Iraqi border, this information was not good news, and morale suffered as a result of it. I prayed that President Bush would just say "Enough!" so that we could get on with it. Both the Bravo and Charlie companies were packed and ready, as were the FRSS and STP groups. All we needed was President Bush's order telling us to go. We knew we could not sustain our battle against low unit morale forever.

Our spirits were somewhat lifted when we learned of a meeting to be held among the United States, Spain, and the United Kingdom. They would be discussing the integration of forces that would join together to destroy the brutal regime of Saddam Hussein despite the lack of endorsement by other nations that were members of the Security Council. We viewed this as a very positive step, and it energized us. We really did not care about the political wrangling and how war would ultimately be declared. We simply just wanted to get on with it.

We firmly believed in the words of President Bush when he said, "Saddam Hussein has gone to elaborate lengths, spent enormous sums, taken great risks to build and keep weapons of mass destruction. . . . The only possible explanation, the only possible use he could have for those weapons, is to dominate, intimidate, or attack." We believed we had existed and survived for solely one reason, which was to fight and support a war on terrorism that would provide a more secure and protected nation—our true home, the United States of America.

Along with President Bush and our many loved ones at home, we too prayed for God's blessings and placed our confidence in a loving God who would guide us in doing the right thing.

# 11

# HEIGHTENED ALERT
# AND FINAL PREPARATIONS

O n Monday, 17 March, we received information that President
Bush was scheduled to address the American nation in a televised speech at 9 PM EST (Tuesday, 18 March, 4 AM Kuwaiti time).
Throughout the day, we speculated about what our commander in
chief would say and hoped he would be declaring war. Our fighting
troops were prepared and ready to begin the quest of liberating Baghdad. All companies, platoons, and groups of the Second FSSG were
also ready to provide these frontline fearless warriors with the highest
quality of medical care we could offer.

Instead of a declaration of war, however, the primary purpose of
the president's speech that night was to give Saddam Hussein and his
sons one final ultimatum—either leave Iraq within forty-eight hours,
or the military would take action. None of us expected that either Hussein or his sons would leave, so we used this forty-eight-hour period to
complete final preparations for not only moving north into Iraq but
also ensuring our own personal safety.

We practiced Scud-alert drills. Whenever the alarm sounded, we
grabbed our Alice packs that contained MOPP gear and our web belts

with gas masks, helmets, goggles, and pistol attached and made a mad dash to the closest Scud bunker. These bunkers consisted of nothing more than a plywood-framed shed reinforced with sandbags stacked on the roof and around its sides. They were imbedded approximately four feet into the sand, and we needed to descend three to four sand-bag steps into a trench to gain access to one of the entryways located on either side of the bunker. Once inside, we had ample headroom to stand, and depending on the number of people entering the bunker, we could use floor room to crouch down on the sandy deck. More often than not, however, the bunker's interior provided standing room only for the twenty to thirty folks who would take refuge.

The Scud bunkers were dark, dank, crowded, and claustrophobic. We could not see outside because the bunkers did not have windows and because the doors provided little more than a view of the entry trench where the sandbag steps were located. After my first visit to one of the bunkers, I found I could not tolerate the inability to see what was happening around me, now an instinct for me since that frightful nighttime invasion of my apartment in Orlando. As a result, I would take partial cover within the bunker's entry trench at the base of the sandbag steps where I could see the sky and feel more in control of my surroundings and even my own death. Being crushed and buried alive should the bunker take a direct hit or collapse from the vibration of nearby explosions was not a desirable death to me, and although I was more exposed to possibly being wounded by shrapnel from exploding ordnance, I was willing to take my chances.

Once the "all clear" signal was sounded, we could remove our gas masks and return to our berthing tents, relieved to be outside of those suffocating, dark bunkers. Little did we know during this prewar prac-tice period just how frequently we would be required to seek refuge in and around these crowded plywood-and-sandbag enclosures.

Packing Alice packs and seabags for the final time was challenging and difficult. We had spent countless hours anticipating, evaluating, and identifying items that would be essential for survival. Now that we were on the brink of war, we once again assessed the contents of the Alice packs, which would serve as our sole source of sustenance for three to five days of travel and desert living. What should be packed? What items could be left behind? What would be essential for our personal survival? What could I take that might also be needed to help save the lives of others? We had no previous experience on which to base our decisions; we simply did the best we could.

Having packed and repacked this backpack numerous times, I learned quickly that no space could be wasted. We were issued a three-day ration of meals, which consisted of nine MRE packets. We removed the various food substances from the packets and traded with one another, selecting and packing just the foods we knew we would consume. Because we would be wearing one set of MOPP gear when we entered Iraq and its protective nature wore off after a few days, we were issued a second set, which was to be included in the pack. Because the MREs and MOPP gear took up almost all of the room in the Alice pack, I made a decision not to pack this second MOPP gear set. This was a personal choice and one that I did not share with anyone.

My decision not to pack the MOPP gear was based on my personal desire not to survive a chemical or biological event if one should occur in our future. I believed that few, if any, would truly be able to survive such an event with or without MOPP gear protection. Even if death did not occur instantly from the chemical or biological agents, everything, including our meals and water supply, would be contaminated, and therefore death would still come, this time, though, as a result of starvation. I knew I would rather die within the first minutes of such an attack, no matter how horrific, instead of dying slowly from starvation or the gradual wasting away from exposure to these agents. I was firm in my decision to simply take my chances. By doing so I had more room to pack items I considered essential not only to sustain my own life but also the lives of others. My Alice pack was filled to the brim with MRE items, a few energy bars, a clean T-shirt, and two pairs of running shorts that I discovered worked better for me than cotton underwear. I also included a collapsible Jackson Reese/Mapleson Ambu bag, endotracheal tubes, and a variety of oral and nasal pharyngeal airways that might benefit and possibly save the lives of those we would encounter as we made our way into Iraq.

On 18 March we were given an opportunity to make one three-minute stateside phone call using the camp's only Meridian satellite phone. The enlisted personnel of Bravo Company were given the first opportunity to use the phone, and then the officers would join the line. The wait to use the phone required standing in line for an average of one hour. We all took into account the time difference between Iraq and the United States and tried to gauge the best time we believed we would be able to connect with our loved ones back home. This was a difficult challenge for many because they wanted to talk with not only their spouses but also their children, most of whom would be in school.

I felt it was crucial for me to contact my sister, and I wondered whether this would be the last phone call I would ever make. I could not help but reflect on those who were in the planes or in the World Trade Center towers on 11 September 2001, wondering how they must have felt and what they were thinking when they made their last cell phone call to their loved ones. They did not know whether they were going to die but believed it was a definite possibility. I deeply empathized with those poor souls and believed I was experiencing some of the same feelings of finality they must have felt that horrible day. We expected to be at war in the next few hours. The marines had moved right up to the Iraqi border in preparation to advance and attack. We would follow in their wake, and we all knew our own survival was not guaranteed. The likelihood that we might easily be killed was inherent in the unpredictability and violence of war, and I desperately needed to hear Jeryl's voice one last time. If I were to die during this war, I wanted to die having heard her voice resonate in my heart and mind and to have her last memory of me be my saying "I love you."

The process of using the phone was regulated and strictly monitored. Only two people were allowed in the tent at one time: the person making the call and the person next in line. The security personnel monitoring the phone would listen in on the call, ensuring that we did not relay where we were, where we were going, or what we were about to do. The feeling of desperation was blatantly evident on everyone's face as they waited their turn to use the phone. Departing the tent after making their brief three-minute call, they were either smiling and rejoicing that they had been able to talk with their loved ones or crying in disappointment that they either ended up leaving a message or were able to talk only to their spouse and not to their school-age children.

When my time arrived to make a call, I was able to connect only with Jeryl's cell phone voice mail. Instead of wasting my one allotted and possibly last phone call of my life in the form of a message, I quickly hung up and returned to the end of the line to wait for another opportunity. My second attempt to reach her, this time by calling her direct line at her place of work, also resulted in failure. We had only a twenty-four-hour opportunity to use the phone, but when my third try to contact Jeryl resulted again in receiving her voice mail, I once again refused to waste my call by talking to a machine. I needed to talk with another human being, and I needed to do so before the Meridian phone was no longer available to us.

I doubted that my mother would fully understand where I was or what I was experiencing. I decided instead to attempt to contact a friend I had known for years. I knew my good friend Capt. Sandra "Sam" Yerkes, a navy psychiatrist, would probably be at her desk working at the Bureau of Medicine and Surgery in Washington, D.C. The phone rang, and Sam picked up. I was so delighted to hear her voice; it warmed my heart. Instead of the impersonal mechanical voice of an answering machine or voice mail, I was talking with someone in the States, something I had been deprived of doing for more than a month.

Sam said, "Cheryl, are you okay? What do you need?"

"I need you to call Jeryl and tell her that I love her," I responded.

Without hesitating a moment, Sam said, "I will. I'll call her as soon as we hang up. Do you need anything?"

I told Sam I could use cereal, dried fruit, Kool-Aid, Sweet'N Low packets, and some Motrin. When I told her I needed the Motrin, she exclaimed, "Motrin! You're at a freaking hospital, Cheryl!" That's when I knew she did not fully understand the situation I was in, where acquiring a small supply of Motrin would entail traveling twenty minutes across the desert to where Alpha Company was holding sick call. The trip was not only potentially dangerous but also totally dependent on finding transportation, which was not an easy task to accomplish. All of our Bravo Surgical Company hospital gear, medications, and supplies were already tightly packed and secured in the ISO containers ready to be deployed forward, and even if we could have accessed them, our medication supply was being saved for those who might need them more, those who were injured in the war.

I did not have time during my precious three minutes of "talk time" to explain the logistical challenge of acquiring Motrin on-site and that, although I was at a hospital, our wartime mobile surgical hospital/trauma unit was not anything like a hospital stateside. I felt frustrated, even a little desperate, and began to wonder whether my letters to my friends were being received. In all the letters I had sent to family and friends, I had tried to describe how we were living and what we were forced to endure. I asked Sam whether she and others were receiving my letters, and she assured me they were arriving and were being read. I wondered again whether perhaps some of the confusion and inability to understand the stark circumstances and environment at Camp Guadalcanal was a result of the CNN broadcasts made from those other more modern and civilized camps. We did not have any imbedded journalists in our group at that time, and as a result, no reports or televised images were shown of our small, stark, sand berm–rimmed tent camp.

I felt frustrated not being able to explain all this to Sam fully, and as my precious three minutes came to a close, I begged her to just please call my family and tell them that I loved them and that I was very thankful for everything they did for me. The last thing I said to her was, "Please make sure my flag is flown for my retirement and give my love to all my friends."

Our conversation had been so short and perfunctory, yet I felt so good about being able to talk to and hear the voice of a caring and compassionate friend. My spirits were lifted, and I exited the tent with a smile on my face and a genuinely warm feeling inside.

With heightened spirits, I returned to my berthing tent for a night of rest. I believed I had accomplished all that I could; I had informed and reassured my family and friends that I loved them and that I was doing okay. Feeling relieved, I believed I was now more than ready to deal with the future, even when that future promised the unpredictable, chaotic world of war.

Our daily routine of musters, anesthesia society meetings, classes, and physical exercise that we had established and maintained throughout our thirty-one days in Kuwait was quickly replaced by the accelerated activities required for moving into Iraq. Ambulances were lined up and staged within the camp for forward deployment. Farewells and best wishes were extended to the members of the FRSS and STP groups as they departed for their staging area.

The mission and location for our three surgical hospital companies had been established, and final preparations were being made. Alpha Company would maintain its operation and location in Kuwait at Camp Okinawa, approximately ten miles from our present location of Camp Guadalcanal. They would receive the first casualties sustained when the marines crossed the border into Iraq. Once the marines moved farther north to secure the area and provide safer passage, Charlie Company would move into the southernmost region of Iraq and set up operations at Camp Viper near the oil fields in Al Bashra. A few days later, Bravo Company would move even farther north beyond Al Bashra to set up operations close to Al Diwaniyah, where resistance and heavy fighting from Saddam's elite Republican Guard were anticipated. The fighting was expected to be fierce and bloody and could easily result in numerous casualties on both sides.

These three locations, one in Kuwait and two in southern Iraq, were the initial areas we were to travel, and they were to be temporary.

The overall plan for the three mobile surgical hospital companies called for each to pack up after stabilizing and transferring the military wounded to an expeditionary medical facility (EMF) such as the USNS *Comfort* or the Army Regional Medical Center in Landstuhl, Germany. Wounded EPWs would be treated, stabilized, and transferred to local civilian hospitals. Once all patients had been transferred and the fighting moved closer to Baghdad, the hospital located the farthest south would move forward to a location closest to the fighting. This move was referred to as "leap-frog advancement."

It was expected that although Bravo Company would take the initial forward lead north of Camp Viper where Charlie Company was stationed in Iraq, Alpha Company would treat, stabilize, and transfer the initial war wounded, pack up and depart its location in northern Kuwait to "leap" farther north ahead of both forward companies, and set up again closest to the major area of battle. If needed, Charlie Company would then leap forward beyond Alpha Company, and the leap-frog advancement would continue as needed. This plan would ensure that at least one surgical hospital would be readily and immediately accessible to treat and care for the wounded as the war advanced forward. Unfortunately, as we would soon learn, planning for the medical needs of the wounded was one thing, but the actual execution of that plan during the chaos and unpredictability of war would be another matter.

Transportation plans for moving personnel and equipment into Iraq were tentative, unreliable, and dependent on the needs of our fighting forces. Once the war began, certain modes of transportation might be needed elsewhere and therefore no longer available to us. Transport of company personnel via C-130 planes was not a sure thing, so we received a special "convoy briefing" to prepare us for travel via truck convoys.

Convoy travel through the exposed, barren desert of Iraq was risky and extremely dangerous. These long lines of slow-moving seven-ton trucks were highly vulnerable to enemy attack. We were instructed to warn any civilians approaching the trucks to move back. The warning was to be given only once, and if they did not comply, we were to keep moving forward even if that meant we would drive over them. We were told that if a truck ahead of us should break down, we should pass it and stay together with the other moving vehicles. Should our own truck break down, we should disembark from the vehicle as quickly as possible and form a 360-degree circle around the vehicle with our backs to it so that we would be able to watch all sides for any approaching enemy or threat. We were also to ensure that our weapons were at the ready. If repair to the vehicle could not be completed quickly, we were to abandon it and all the contents within. Little did we know at the time we received this instruction the impact that convoy travel would ultimately have on our abilities to render care to our troops.

We believed we were mere hours from a declaration of war on Iraq. We had immersed ourselves in a flurry of prewar activity, including packing, repacking, bidding farewell to our battle buddies, making the one brief three-minute phone call stateside, and receiving last-minute essential survival training. In an instant, our life at Camp Guadalcanal was completely changed, and the changes were eerie.

The camp's chow hall was especially quiet the evening of 19 March, less than eight hours before President Bush was expected to declare war. This special place, where we had spent hours bantering, joking, discussing mundane silly events and issues, and sharing our successes, failures, and frustrations, was now quiet and devoid of many familiar faces from the FRSS and STP groups. Most of us sat silently, lost in our own thoughts as we ate our meals.

As I settled into my sleeping bag that night, I thought of my home and family in the States. I also thought about the average poor-income Iraqi family and wondered how they must be feeling tonight. Were they afraid for their lives and those of their children? Would they be safe? Would any of us be truly safe in this war of unknowns?

# 12

# WAR IS DECLARED

On the morning of 20 March 2003, at 5:45 AM Kuwaiti time (19 March, 9:45 PM EST), the first U.S. missiles were launched into Iraq. War had officially been declared between the American-led coalition forces and Iraq. Operation Iraqi Freedom had officially begun!

We received this long-awaited definitive news at breakfast. The atmosphere throughout the chow tent that morning was exceptionally quiet and subdued. Some of us sat silently, lost in our personal thoughts, while others tried diligently to obtain additional information from portable hand radios. We were anxious and apprehensive but also eager. We were on the brink of war, and as some sat silently, fearing for their lives, I was eager to move on and thought, "Finally! It's about time! Now, when do we leave?" Once again we were haunted with questions and doubts about whether we knew enough to provide the needed medical care to our wounded troops. This fear surrounding the adequacy of our preparedness to render care to the wounded was more prevalent than the fear for our own lives.

The quiet stillness of our camp was short lived. Just as I completed my three-minute rinse-off shower around 10 AM, I heard the first Scud alert. I immediately grabbed my gear (Alice pack, web belt with gas mask, helmet with goggles, and pistol) that I carried with me wherever I went and ran for the cover of the Scud bunkers. This was the first of seventeen alerts we would experience in the first twenty hours of war. Ultimately, we endured fifty Scud missile alarms during the days we remained in Kuwait.

Scud alerts had no pattern and would be sounded anytime throughout the day and night. Our sleep was often interrupted several times on many successive nights. At times we would no sooner return to our tents from one alert than the alarm would sound again. Procedure called for Scud alerts to be sounded immediately upon missile detection and four minutes before their intercept. This procedure was not always followed because the frequency of Scud detection was often much less than four minutes. One Scud missile was so unexpected and so close that the explosion from it being intercepted by a Patriot missile violently threw us from our cots as we attempted to sleep. No alarm had been sounded.

Each time the alarm sounded, we raced to the bunkers, attired in Kevlar vests, helmets, and goggles. Carrying our Alice packs, we would often don our gas masks as we ran. Just as in our practice sessions, we would scramble down the sandbag steps, enter the doorway of these crude plywood/sandbag shelters, and, along with the twenty-plus others who were seeking cover, crouch or stand, tightly packed together, anywhere from fifteen to forty-five minutes. And just like during practice, these bunkers were hot and uncomfortable. We had little more to do than breathe in the desert sand and taste our own fear as it welled up in the back of our throats.

Because we were required to seek shelter so frequently, many of us soon established our favorite bunker and our own spot either within or just outside of the bunker's entryway. Knowing who usually selected a certain bunker and where they routinely crouched or stood was helpful because it provided us with the ability to visually check that everyone had made it to the bunker safely.

Even though these alerts were now real and not just drills, I continued to remain in my usual position, standing in the trench just outside the bunker's entryway where I could see what was going on around me. From my vantage point I could easily see the explosions created by Patriot missiles intercepting incoming Scuds, some as close as a mile and a half away. Red streaks filled the sky, and we had little doubt that the enemy was aiming at all American camps just south of the Iraqi border, including our own. We soon realized that this enemy was not inclined to distinguish between noncombatant medical support personnel and fighting troops; Saddam and his gang of cutthroats wanted to kill *all* Americans, and we, along with the fighting troops, had become nothing more than targets to them.

Within hours after the ground war began at 9:45 PM (Kuwait time) on 20 March, Alpha Surgical Company began receiving casualties. We could see the choppers clearly as they made their way to Alpha's field hospital, a mere ten miles from our Camp Guadalcanal location. At one point we even needed to provide a C-46 helicopter pilot with directions to the Alpha site because he had landed at our location thinking we were set up to care for the wounded.

Word of the nature and severity of the wounded quickly filtered into our camp. Alpha's ORs stayed busy, their personnel trying diligently to repair horrific human damage sustained as a result of multiple gunshots or land mine explosions. The surgical teams were faced with a variety of injuries, ranging from severed aortas and gunshots through the liver to extraction of a small flashlight that had been imbedded into a young marine's chest by the impact of an explosive. The teams were successful in saving the lives of many, yet some of the troops would be too severely wounded to be saved, and would die.

The medical personnel comprising the Alpha Company worked tirelessly those first hours and days of the war, saving as many lives as was humanly possible. We benefited from their experience, and they readily shared with us the lessons they had learned from the administration of care to these first war casualties. Hypothermia was the greatest challenge they had to manage. Keeping the patients warm and maintaining their internal body temperature were critical for survival.

They also shared with us the slight modification in normal triage procedure they enacted specific to dealing with wounded EPWs. Normal or routine triage procedure calls for all casualties to be indiscriminately evaluated on a first-come, first-evaluated basis. Those who had sustained the most serious life-threatening treatable wounds would receive immediate care, whereas those with less-severe injuries would wait and be treated next. Modification to this procedure consisted of a slight delay in the evaluation and treatment of the EPWs if numerous wounded EPWs and American troops were brought into the triage area at the same time. The American troops were evaluated and treated first; once all our troops were rendered care, then evaluation and care for the EPWs was provided. Because the wounding and killing of our American troops was a direct result of EPW actions, this was not a difficult decision, and we all believed it was rational and justified. The medical team of the Bravo Surgical Company readily adopted this wartime triage standard.

On Tuesday, 24 March, Charlie Company personnel were loaded onto C-53 aircraft for their journey to a location near the oil fields of Al Bashra. The members of Charlie Company would be the first of the surgical companies to move into Iraq and would be stationed immediately behind the frontline of this slow-moving war. Their gear, equipment, and supplies were to be transported to this new location via convoy trucks. I felt a deep personal void and sense of loss when they left our small Camp Guadalcanal encampment. I would miss seeing them and could do little more than pray that they would be safe as they ventured into the hostile, foreign, chaotic country of Iraq.

They were entering into a new kind of hell, one that was filled with fire, black smoke, contaminated air, and heavy fighting. Even from our southern location in Kuwait, the sky took on an orange, glazed appearance layered with black smoke and heavy, oily soot created by the blazing oil fields of Al Bashra. The contamination of the air caused our eyes to water and burn. Some even began to experience respiratory wheezing and congestion. Although we had known we were close to the Iraqi border, seeing this orange-streaked, black-layered sky and experiencing its contaminating effect demonstrated just how close we actually were.

Once Charlie Company departed, we knew we would not be far behind; so we continued to ready ourselves for our imminent departure. The day following Charlie Company's departure, we were told that our cots would be collected to be placed into the ISO containers. Once again we would return to sleeping in our sleeping bags on the ground. We were told that Bravo Company would be leaving on Thursday, 27 March, giving us a little more than forty-eight hours before we were to board convoy trucks and begin a thirty-hour journey to an area expected to experience heavy and major casualties.

We were instructed to remove all prized and valued personal possessions, such as photos and letters, from the one seabag that would be transported along with us in a separate truck and to repack these possessions in our Alice packs, which would remain with us at all times. This instruction came after the command learned that one of the seven vehicles transporting Charlie Company's gear, equipment, and personal seabags broke down and needed to be abandoned in transit to Al Bashra. When they returned the following day to retrieve the trucks' contents, the group found that their seabags, tents, and much of the hospital equipment had been stolen. Those in Charlie Company were now forced to sleep, eat, and live in the open without any kind of shelter from the wind, rain, and cold night temperatures of this barren land. Their ability to provide medical care and support to the injured troops had been compromised, and many of their cherished personal possessions were gone forever.

As instructed, I chose one personal and cherished item to transfer from my seabag into my Alice pack. That item was an angel given to me by my sister. This angel gave me comfort and represented the deep love my sister and I shared for one another. In my helmet I placed one letter I had received from each family member and one from each of my friends. Knowing that we would probably not receive mail for a long time once we entered Iraq, I wanted to have these letters with me to read and reread, for they provided me with comfort and a sense of home.

On Thursday, 27 March, at 6 PM we were notified that instead of leaving Camp Guadalcanal as anticipated, we were ordered to report to the ISO containers to remove one OR and a ward (tents, OR table, cots, supplies, equipment, and so on) and place them on a pallet. This equipment was to be airlifted to Camp Viper to augment the equipment and supplies that had been stolen from Charlie Company's abandoned convoy truck. This grueling work took more than five hours to complete. We had to be meticulous in our efforts, ensuring that everything was packed, arranged, and distributed evenly and in accordance with the aircraft's airlift capabilities. At 11 PM we finally completed our task, and we returned to our tents exhausted and craving an opportunity to rest in between the Scud alerts that continued to plague us.

The following morning, no further word was given about our departure time, so I planned to complete a run around the perimeter of the berm following breakfast. These plans were quickly put aside when we were informed at muster that we needed to remove everything we had placed on the pallets the evening before and load it all back into our ISO containers. The word we received was that those in Charlie Company had located their lost equipment and would not need the massive amount of equipment that comprised an OR, a ward, and an ancillary unit. Once again, we began the arduous chore of packing the ISO containers that we would be taking with us when we moved into Iraq.

Just as we were completing this six-hour, backbreaking task, several trucks arrived with orders to load and transport one OR, one ward, and an ancillary unit for use by Charlie Company, now located at Camp Viper. We were all very frustrated with this mess we were experiencing and quickly labeled it a "cluster fuck." None of us had ever seen this degree of miscommunication that required so much strenuous work, only for it to end up being meaningless. Still, we overcame our bitter feelings of frustration, anger, and exhaustion and moved into action, unloading and reloading containers that would send much of our own company's essential surgical and medical equipment to Camp Viper.

We had packed, unpacked, and repacked the hospital equipment three times in less than forty-eight hours. Although it was a frustrating and maddening endeavor, it also brought the personnel of Bravo Company closer together, and we grew as a team, developing respect for and awareness of our individual capabilities and the various levels of expertise we possessed outside the medical/surgical arena. We now knew who was capable of lifting the heavier items, who had spatial acumen and could direct the placement of the various items into the ISO containers so they could be unloaded in a logical and efficient manner, and who had what level of endurance. Although we did not realize it at the time, having to perform this loading, unloading, loading, unloading "cluster" evolution would serve us well once we journeyed into Iraq.

The theft of convoy contents and the relentless threat of Scud missiles were not our only concern. Within days of the start of the war, we received security briefings and reports that the enemy was stealing American military uniforms with the intent to infiltrate our bases and that Iraqi soldiers were posing as civilians. We countered this threat by devising strategies to help us readily identify our enemy.

Each day we were given three different security passwords. At any time, those three passwords could be asked of us, and if an individual did not say those precise words, that person was immediately considered a threat. We were instructed to yell to the potential enemy with our hand palm out and our arm extended in front (similar to the motion a traffic cop would use to stop traffic) to "halt" or "stop." If the individual refused to stop approaching us, we were to use our pistol to shoot to kill. We were also briefed on the various tattoos that many Iraqi guerrilla forces sported to indicate their loyalty to Saddam or their membership in the Republican Guard, Baath Party, fedayeen, or other hostile enemy group.

Most important, we were to be ever vigilant and cognizant of who was in the camp, whether everyone looked familiar, and whether anyone was acting suspicious in anyway. This vigilance was especially critical because we continued to have civilians coming into the camp to deliver food. It was impossible to know whether one of these civilians was possibly an enemy spy, so we were told not to talk when we went to the food-serving tent to get our food. The basic motto we lived by was "Trust no one you do not know."

Suicide bombers were everywhere, ramming the gates of our camps and our security checkpoints and readily destroying our convoys. Americans were being maimed and destroyed by enemy soldiers posing as U.S. military personnel or as helpless civilians. We were all vulnerable to these subversive, covert attacks. I had once questioned my resolve to take the life of another and had found it a concept too overwhelming and too far-fetched to even contemplate. I had consciously chosen not to think about it or to process it when General Conway spoke to us less than a month prior.

Over time, however, as I began to truly realize the realities of this war and the tactics being used by the Iraqi soldiers, my anger toward them grew stronger and would soon turn to hate. This harsh, deep-seated feeling, combined with fear for myself and others and my determination to survive, would eventually allow me to have no doubt. Should I become threatened or if the life of one of my battle buddies should become jeopardized, I knew with certainty that I could and would kill the enemy without reservation.

Jeryl and I dressed alike as "twins."

Photo taken of me just prior to entering nursing school.

My cousin Kathy and I, 1996.

*Left to right,* Capt. Gordon Cornell, then–Lt. Cheryl Ruff, and Lt. Cdr. Shirley Cornell.

Lt. Cdr. Cheryl L. Ruff,
U.S. Navy Nurse Corps.

Relaxing at "home" in Camp Guadalcanal, Kuwait, February 2003.

Dressed in full gear that
weighed sixty pounds.

Taking a break at "home" outside OR number two, Camp Anderson, Iraq.

View from the bed of our seven-ton truck during convoy ride to Camp Chesty.

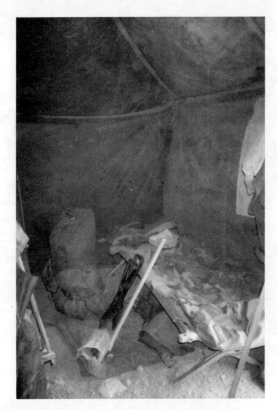

"Home sweet home" in Camp Chesty, Iraq.

With Lt. Cdr. Necia Williams, Camp Chesty, Iraq; we finally got a chance to wash our hair.

Bravo Surgical Company bids farewell to CNN photographer "Mad Dog" and medical reporter Dr. Sanjay Gupta.

Working with Lt. Cdr. Dave Sheppard in OR number two, Camp Chesty, Iraq.

Reunited with friend Cdr. Vanessa Noggle at Camp Okinawa, Kuwait.

Reunited with my sister, Jeryl, at home in Portsmouth, Virginia.

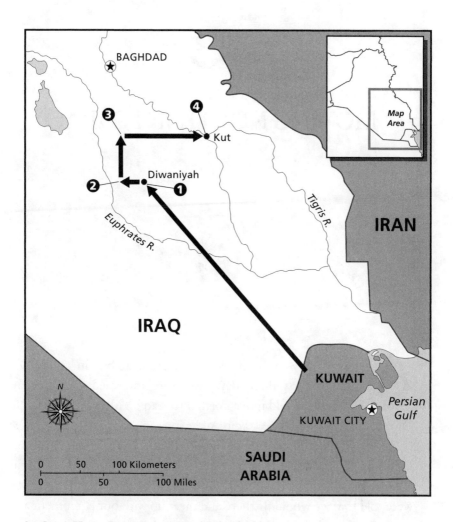

1. Camp Hasty, Diwaniyah. Arrived 2 April 2003.

2. Camp Anderson, about twenty miles west of Diwaniyah. Arrived 3 April 2003.

3. Camp Chesty, about forty miles north of Camp Anderson and about seventy miles south of Baghdad. Arrived 7 April 2003.

4. Camp Geiger, on the outskirts of Al Kut. Arrived 25 April 2003.

# 13

## MOVING NORTH INTO IRAQ

A fter waiting what seemed like an eternity, but in reality was a total of forty-three days, we were informed on Saturday, 29 March, that we would move north into Iraq on Monday, 31 March. Our destination would be Camp Anderson, an area twenty miles west of Al Diwaniyah and about one hundred miles from Baghdad. Heavy fighting was expected in this area because the new moon would occur 1 April, creating ideal conditions for our American troops to fight. We were told that we would fly there and meet up with our equipment and that we would then need to hit the ground running, immediately setting up our makeshift trauma center to be ready to receive incoming casualties. Because one of our ORs, a ward, and an ancillary unit had been detailed to Camp Viper, we were to meet up with two FRSS units that would augment Camp Anderson with their two ORs and a few surgeons and ICU personnel. The combination of the FRSS surgical teams and the Bravo Surgical Company would provide greater surgical operating capabilities in this area in the event the casualties were as numerous as anticipated.

Our equipment and gear, packed in the ISO containers, were loaded onto trucks and began their northward journey via convoy. We could not help but wonder whether we would ever see our precious medical/surgical equipment, supplies, gear, and personal seabags again or whether this cargo would suffer the same fate of being abandoned and stolen en route as Charlie Company's was. A few Bravo Company personnel accompanied the ISO container convoy. These personnel included the executive officer, the chief nurse, and some administrative enlisted. They were to arrive early in Camp Anderson to survey the terrain and plan the logistical setup and placement of the various tents (triage, ORs, and ICU) that made up our mobile surgical hospital. We would need to set up quickly once we all arrived at this camp, so advanced logistical planning was critical.

On Sunday we attended Protestant worship service and then what we thought would be our final briefing at Camp Guadalcanal. During this time we were divided into "stix" for the purpose of being loaded onto the transport helicopters (CH-53). Stix were alphabetical groupings of twenty to twenty-four individuals. Each stix was then given a number, and we would board the choppers when our stix number was called. I was in stix number six.

That evening we enjoyed our "last supper" in Kuwait. We talked, we joked, we laughed, and we offered spirited words of encouragement to one another. Our spirits were high, for we were all looking forward to moving on and out of Kuwait. Our thinking remained the same as always; we believed the sooner we started, the sooner the mission could be completed and the sooner we would return to our homes in the United States.

I retired early that night, expecting to rise at 4 AM to pack the last few items in preparation for boarding the choppers. I wrote a letter to my sister and completed my daily journal entry. I was so sure we would be going north that, after I finished writing about the day's events, I wrote "IRAQ" across the page in my journal in preparation for the next day's entry. I had no idea what I would be writing about, but I fully expected that the next time I opened my journal I would be in Iraq.

The following day I found myself using my pen to scratch through the "IRAQ" heading I had previously written in my journal. We were not going anywhere on 31 March because we "did not have a security force in place"; at least that is what we were told at muster. Whatever the reason, we were to remain in Kuwait at least one more day. We were placed on "holiday routine," but our mood was anything but festive. We were angry and frustrated, and we used the day to exercise, wash a few clothes, and place bets as to when we might actually leave. We all felt as though we were the recipients of a premature April Fool's joke and hoped the same would not result once 1 April actually arrived.

Reveille was sounded at four o'clock the following morning. We donned our MOPP gear, packed all last-minute items surrounding our berthing spaces, and hoisted our fully loaded Alice packs, along with our sleeping bags, onto our backs. Our canteens, pistols, ammunition, and gas masks were strapped onto our bodies. Loaded with at least sixty pounds of gear, we reported to our 5 AM muster fully expecting to immediately board a transport helicopter that would take us into Iraq.

We arranged ourselves into our assigned stix during muster. As the sun began to rise, so did the stifling temperature, and we soon found ourselves standing in the barren desert sand totally exposed to the hot, oppressive sun and blazing heat. One hour passed, followed by another, and another, and another. We neither saw helicopters anywhere nor heard the familiar whomp-whomp sound of the choppers' rotary blades. There was no shade or shelter available to us, and the MOPP clothing, combined with the heavy Alice pack and gear we wore, intensified our internal body heat. We were all miserable, sweating profusely, and as our bodies began to feel as though they were reaching their boiling points, so followed our temperaments. We were tired, frustrated, and growing increasingly impatient with this stagnant, miserable situation of wait, wait, wait, and wait some more.

No one knew precisely when our transportation would arrive. The choppers could arrive in a matter of minutes or in several hours. As a result, when we needed to go to the job johnnies to relieve ourselves, we first needed to ask our stix leader for permission to do so. It was reminiscent of grade school and slightly humiliating to go up to the stix leader and say, "Chief, can I go pee?" Still, we also understood the importance of the leader knowing our whereabouts at all times in the event the choppers were sighted.

Usually only two battle buddies were allowed to break formation from the stix at any one time. Going to the johnnies and relieving ourselves was an arduous task in itself. It was impossible to simply drop your drawers without first taking off the sixty-pound-plus Alice pack and other gear. The pack and weapons would be left outside the john under the watchful eye of your battle buddy.

Within our eight different stix, we were lined up like little ants, and we remained standing for hours. No food had been brought into the camp because we were not expected to still be there. The food providers had been told that we would be well on our way to Iraq and that food delivery to our camp would no longer be required. As the noon hour approached, it became essential for us to be provided with nourishment from a source other than the nine MREs we had in our Alice packs. That food would be the only means we had to survive for the three days immediately after we left Kuwait. That food should not be consumed before we even left a place where another source of sustenance was available. Eventually, action was taken so that we were given lunch sandwiches and a dinner meal, which were brought to us by the Kuwaiti civilians.

At 5:30 PM, twelve hours after we had formed into our stix, we were told we could go to one of the empty tents to consume our dinner. We were given fifteen minutes to eat, and only two stix groups were allowed to go at any one time. It was close to 7 PM by the time my stix was finishing dinner, and the sky was growing dark. We knew the choppers would not be flying at night to transport medical personnel into Iraq, especially because Scud-missile traffic was so heavy during the twilight and nighttime hours.

Disregarding the fifteen minutes we were allowed, we took our time consuming our meals, and when we did return to the staging

area, we sat around some more. At 8 PM we were told that we could
return to our berthing tents to rest and that we needed to plan for an
early flight out the following day. Once again it seemed that we were
on the receiving end of yet another April Fool's joke. This time our
delay was a result of headquarters failing to validate the manifest for
our flight into Iraq. The reason did not matter much to me. It had
been a very tiring, useless, and frustrating eighteen-hour day, and all
I could do was hope and pray that 2 April would prove to be more
positive.

Although we had been told to expect a 5 AM reveille, we were awakened at 3:30 AM on 2 April. Two C-130 marine cargo planes had
landed outside the Alpha Company's camp and were waiting for us to
board for transport into Iraq. We loaded onto five-ton trucks for the
nearly thirty-minute ride to the planes. It was a rough ride, but bear-
able. At least we were finally going somewhere, although we did wonder how long we would be waiting this time before we actually
boarded our transport into Iraq. After experiencing the frustration,
delay, and misery of waiting all throughout the previous day and going
nowhere other than back to our berthing tents, we were very skeptical,
and our trust in the system was shaky at best.

We began boarding chronologically according to our assigned stix
number. We walked up the rear loading ramp of the plane and planted
ourselves anywhere we could on the plane's floor, sitting on our
packs. A total of ninety-six of us were smashed like sardines within the
plane's interior for the ninety-minute flight to Al Diwaniyah. The slightest movement by anyone for the purpose of relieving a leg or arm
cramp or trying to obtain a more comfortable position would invariably
cause major discomfort and even pain to those wedged in alongside that
person.

The plane was forced to make severe turns and take an erratic flight
pattern to avoid being a target for the enemy's ground-to-air missiles.
The heat within the plane, combined with the cramped conditions and

constant swerving motion, caused many people to become airsick, and they began vomiting onto themselves and, in many cases, onto their neighboring battle buddy. I was one of the last ones to board the plane and had the luxury of sitting on the mailbags at the very tail end of the plane's cargo hold. I found that it was one of the better places within the plane to be situated because I could look out one of the small portholes. Being able to look out helped to curb my own nauseous feeling, and I felt very fortunate.

At 10:00 AM we descended, and the plane landed just outside Al Diwaniyah on what was once a highway and was now a makeshift airstrip. We had arrived at Camp Hasty, a desolate place offering very little security, no shelter, and no bathroom facilities. As soon as the plane landed and the rear ramp door was opened, all we could hear was people shouting, "Get out, get out!" We needed to disembark quickly so the plane could become airborne again and not serve as a stationary target for the enemy.

As I ran down the plane's lowered rear ramp, images I had seen on television of troops entering South Vietnam came to mind. Instead of watching it, I was living it, and it was a very eerie, surreal experience. The first thing I noticed was a green grassy area, something I had not seen since I left the United States. Off in the far distance I could also see a few palm trees. I was so awestruck by this greenery, something I had been deprived of seeing for almost two months, that I thought little about the fact that I was placing my foot into a country on which we had declared war. It was such a stark contrast from the miles and miles of nothing but sand that we had viewed every day from our camp in the Kuwaiti desert.

As soon as we disembarked from the plane we were directed to an area far back from the landing strip and behind a road that was bordered by palm trees. The area was interspersed with some grass, a lot of dirt, and some scraggly sage shrubs. We were told that we needed to stay together as a group in a very precise and specified area and that our bathroom facility was a small, adjacent, open-exposed area containing nothing, again, but dirt and a few sage shrubs. We were sternly warned not to go beyond this specified area because anything beyond its boundaries had not been cleared of land mines, and therefore our safety could not be assured.

Any semblance of bathroom privacy we once might have had was left far behind at Camp Guadalcanal. Now that we had entered Iraq, it mattered little where and when we would drop our drawers for the purpose of relieving our bowels or our bladders or even changing our tampons. There was no room on the battlefield for such luxuries as modesty or even real privacy. That which we had once considered to be a big deal in our own country had now become a non-issue for us, especially considering that our lives were very much in jeopardy.

We had landed at this place called Camp Hasty, which was nothing more than a relatively "secure" small plot of dirt and gravel land, to wait for choppers to transport us farther north to Camp Anderson. We were told that land travel was too dangerous a mode and that we needed to wait for helicopter transport. The sun was blazing overhead, and because we continued to be fully attired in our MOPP gear, we all felt hot and miserable, and we were trying desperately to recuperate from the residual airsickness symptoms caused by the hot, cramped, and ever-swerving flight of the C-130s.

At 2:30 PM, more than four hours after our arrival, two five-ton trucks arrived to begin transporting us to Camp Anderson via ground transport. Even though we had been told that land travel was danger-ous, it apparently had become even more urgent that we be trans-ported immediately from the vicinity of Camp Hasty. We couldn't wait for air transportation; time was of the essence. Although a few combat marines had set up web tenting and were there to guard this area, they were small in number, and a full-force attack by the enemy could eas-ily result in disaster. Camp Hasty was simply a temporary stop, a place for us to wait for further transportation, and it was becoming more and more obvious to us that we needed to get out of there as expeditiously as possible.

The two five-ton transport trucks accommodated a maximum capacity of thirty people, and once the first thirty were loaded, the two trucks quickly rumbled away, heading north. The rest of us returned to our various perches on the dirt, where we would await the return of the trucks after they off-loaded the first group. At 4:30 PM, six and one-half hours after arriving on the desolate and exposed terrain of Camp Hasty, three CH-46s (small helicopters) arrived, and several members of our group boarded to begin their short journey to Camp Anderson. That left just seventy of us, and when the choppers did not return by 5:30 PM from what was a short five- to ten-minute flight to Camp Anderson, we began to doubt that we would be going anywhere anytime soon.

We watched the marines who were guarding the area begin to pack up, and we still had no indication that we were going to be transported. At 6 PM we were told that we would be staying the night in this godforsaken place, so as darkness fell on us, we pulled out our sleeping bags, huddled down very close to one another, and prepared to spend the night. We doubted that we would be able to sleep because we were also told to "get ready for the fireworks." Although we did not know what that comment meant, before long it became very apparent.

I had no sooner settled in my sleeping bag than I experienced the need to relieve myself. I asked Lt. Cdr. Dave Sheppard, a fellow nurse anesthetist, if he would go with me to the bush area that was our designated bathroom, and he agreed. (We had truly entered into the "gender-neutral" aspect of war, where a battle buddy was a battle buddy and the sex of our buddy made absolutely no difference.) Flashlights were strictly forbidden, so we blindly made our way over to the "bathroom" in total darkness, did our business, and managed to find our way back without stumbling over too many of our sleeping shipmates.

Shortly after we had returned and crawled into our sleeping bags, we saw Apache helicopters at a distance begin firing their missiles. We could easily see the streaks of missile fire and hear the explosions when the missiles found their targets. The sky was filled with red streaks of missile fire; the fireworks show we had been told about had obviously begun.

Within fifteen minutes of the commencement of these fireworks, we heard frantic shouts: "Everybody, get up! Get up! Get your packs! They are coming to get us! Hurry!" We immediately scrambled out of our sleeping bags and began to quickly reassemble our sixty pounds of

gear. We were all exhausted, frustrated, hungry, thirsty, and disori-
ented. The whole area was pitch-dark except for the illumination from
the explosions we could see on the horizon. We were in total chaos, yet
we helped each other as much as we could and made our way to the
piece of road that was also the makeshift airstrip our plane had landed
on earlier.

It was now 9:30 PM, and we could do nothing but stand there near
this airstrip, out in the open, totally exposed. We saw no planes, no
choppers, no aircraft of any kind. Eventually, a few ambulances drove
up, but not nearly enough to transport all seventy of us. Some of the
company members were loaded into the ambulances, but instead of
driving off as we expected, the ambulances simply sat there on the
road, waiting. We were then informed that additional trucks would be
coming to take all of us, via convoy, to Camp Anderson. Despite waiting almost twelve hours for air transportation because land travel had
been determined to be too dangerous, we were now going to travel by
convoy through unsafe territory in total darkness.

Several five-ton trucks arrived around 11 PM, and we were told,
"Get on the trucks. We don't care which truck you get on, just get on
one, and get on now!" There were no seats in the beds of the trucks
and no canvas tarps or canopies covering them. Riding in these open
truck beds, we would be totally exposed to the environment. We
helped each other load our gear into the trucks first, and then we
climbed on board. Our packs and gear would serve as our seats.

Being one of the last to climb aboard, I sat wherever I could,
which was at the back of the truck on top of a large pile of gear.
Perched on this pile of gear my silhouette extended well above the side
of the truck bed, and I knew I was clearly visible and a prime target for
an enemy sniper. I remember thinking, "Well, someone could easily
shoot at me, and there is nothing I can do but sit here." There was no
place else for me to sit, for once again we were smashed into this small
compartment like sardines, and the slightest movement would cause
those next to us significant discomfort and even pain.

Our twenty-mile trip to Camp Anderson became a three-hour
ride. The trucks were making their way without the benefit of head-

lights, and forward movement was excruciatingly slow. All the while, I sat on top of those bags of gear fully aware that I was a target and that my life could easily be ended in an instant by a single shot from a sniper's rifle. I could do nothing more than think about what my life was all about and how I would survive this. It was the longest ride of my life, and for the first time I truly felt I was in harm's way.

# 14

## CAMP ANDERSON

### *The Other Side of Hell*

We arrived at Camp Anderson at 2 AM on 3 April. Those who had been transported in the first trucks from Camp Hasty at 2 PM the previous day had set up what looked like one or two small tents. We could see very little in the blackness of the night and were told to keep our red-filtered flashlights turned off because snipers had fired at the camp earlier that evening. The early arrivals were spread out in the darkness on the open ground in their sleeping bags, trying to rest.

Too afraid to venture very far for fear of stepping on a land mine and yet needing to empty my painfully full bladder, I jumped off the truck as soon as it stopped and relieved myself right next to it. I then found a spot near the truck's tires and lay down in the dirt dressed in my MOPP gear, armor vest, and helmet, with my pistol at my side. I was exhausted and cold. The bare, damp ground intensified the cold nighttime temperatures. I was freezing and tried to curl up as close as possible to the tires, hoping they still held some warmth from our trip to this other side of hell.

This camp, like the one we had just left, was nothing more than a small area in Iraq that had been designated a "secure area," cleared of land mines. There was no vegetation, or anything else, just a small plot of dirt located next to the road. Across the road from the camp was an area of thick grass, about four feet high. We were told the bodies of several hundred Iraqi soldiers were strewn within the grass as a result of heavy fighting that had taken place the night before. To the rear of the camp was a large pit at least eight feet deep. On the other side of this pit was more thick, tall grass that could easily be used for cover by the approaching enemy.

Of course, we saw little of this when we first arrived that night. Also, our new surroundings were much less important to us than getting some sleep so we could begin setting up our surgical support unit with the dawning of first light.

At 5 AM, after getting no more than three hours of sleep, we got up from our dirt beds and began the chore of setting up tents and equipment that would serve as our combat trauma surgical center. While we toiled at this laborious task, we were able to view more of this new hell into which we had entered.

We could now see the tall grass on the other side of the road and wondered about the dead bodies of the Iraqi soldiers lying there. We also saw the deep pit at the rear of our camp and were told the bathroom was located at the bottom of this pit.

The "bathroom" was nothing more than a hole that had been dug within the pit. This primitive place was where we were expected to squat, relieve ourselves, and move on. There was no privacy and no hand-washing area. To access this latrine you needed to walk slowly and carefully down a steep eight-foot embankment and hope you did not lose your footing and fall. With nothing preventing the enemy from firing down at us from the other side, which was shielded by the border of thick, tall grass, to me this pit was a very unsafe area, and I viewed going down into it as a means of early execution.

After seeing this setup, I quickly came to the decision that there was no way I would be going down there. It was a death trap. When I had to answer the call of nature, I simply found a place on the perimeter of the camp, squatted, and completed the deed. I tried to be as discreet as possible, but occasionally someone would inadvertently approach during these private moments. On seeing me, the person would immediately turn away, and the situation ended up being no big deal for anyone. We all understood that there was no time for feeling embarrassed and that privacy had become nothing more than a concept. We were all human beings with the same bodily functions, we were in the middle of God only knows where, we were at war, and we were there to do everything we could to save the lives of our troops. Nothing else really mattered, least of all bathroom privacy.

Setting up the triage tent, two ORs, and an ICU took four hours to complete. It was grueling, strenuous, labor-intensive work performed beneath a scorching sun. By 10 AM the temperature had risen to 110 degrees, and our clothes were soaked through with sweat. Still, we continued to wear our hot, stifling MOPP gear.

The urgency of the situation and the immediate need to be prepared to receive casualties was real and reinforced by the awareness that one of the FRSS units located at the perimeter of the camp was already in the midst of performing surgery. We needed to set up and assume the care of all incoming wounded so the FRSS could shut down, pack up, and move forward with the marines.

The surgery being performed by the FRSS was on a two-year-old child. The child, along with two Iraqi civilian women and another child, had been kidnapped by Iraqi soldiers and placed in a car with a propane tank strapped to it. Believing that the sight of the women and children riding inside the car would deter the U.S. Marines from firing on it, the Iraqi soldiers attempted to drive this explosive-laden vehicle through a marine barricade.

The civilians were being used as human shields and were nothing more than innocent victims of this vicious war. As the car approached the barricade, the marines ordered it to stop. When it failed to do so, the marines had little choice but to open fire, and the Iraqi soldiers were killed. Fortunately, both women survived. One of the children sustained minor injuries, and the two-year-old suffered severe head injuries from exploding shrapnel.

Dr. Sanjay Gupta, a CNN reporter and skilled neurosurgeon, was at Camp Anderson developing medical news reports to be broadcast on CNN. We did not have a neurosurgeon among our ranks, and Dr. Gupta was asked to assist with the surgery of this gravely injured toddler. Unfortunately, despite six long hours of tedious and delicate surgery, the efforts of the surgical team, headed by Dr. Gupta, proved to be futile. The child did not survive.

By 12:30 PM we had successfully set up the essentials of our surgical trauma unit: a triage tent, two ORs, and an ICU tent. The triage tent was immediately adjacent to an area designated for the landing of the helicopters. To the rear of this tent were the two ORs, with the ICU tent located immediately behind them. A ward tent was still in the process of being erected and would be situated alongside the ICU. This setup provided for quick transfer through the triage tent into one of the ORs, the ICU, or the ward. We scarcely had an opportunity to eat a snack from our MRE packs before the first choppers landed at the camp, carrying the first of the many wounded and dead who would arrive that day.

One after the other those choppers came. It was now my time to take action and do all I could to help save the lives of all those who had been severely and brutally wounded as a result of this cruel and devastating war.

# 15

## SAVING LIVES

As soon as the choppers began to arrive, I was ready to administer anesthesia in OR number two. Both Lieutenant Commander Sheppard, my battle buddy and fellow nurse anesthetist, and I had been assigned as the anesthesia providers for this OR designated to care primarily for those with chest, abdominal, and head injuries. OR number one would care for those who had sustained orthopedic injuries. We knew most of the wounded would have multiple injuries, but if the primary wound had been sustained to the chest, abdomen, or head with secondary wounds sustained to the limbs, the patients would have surgery performed in OR number two. If the primary wound was orthopedic, the individual would have surgery performed in OR number one.

My first patient was an older Iraqi gentleman with multiple gunshots to the abdomen, arm, and leg. These horrendous, bloody wounds had torn deep through his flesh, internal organs, and bones. I performed my first anesthesia procedure using field medical anesthesia equipment that consisted of a vaporizer with tubing that extended from the vaporizer to a mask placed over the patient's nose and mouth.

Midway along the length of this tubing was a reservoir bag that I would manually squeeze in order to provide oxygen and anesthetizing agent/vapors to the patient. In essence, I was breathing for the patient, regulating the inhalation cycle and ventilating him by continuously and rhythmically squeezing the reservoir bag.

The surgeons would work more than six hours on this first patient. They performed an abdominal laparotomy (a surgical incision opening the abdominal cavity) to explore the internal organs for injury or sources of bleeding. Because of injury to the bowel, they needed to perform a bowel resection, which involved excising and removing the damaged portion of the bowel and reconnecting the healthy ends of the upper and lower portions of the bowel to one another. The severe damage to the left brachial artery (the chief blood supply to the arm) would ultimately result in the amputation of the patient's left arm despite the surgeons' painstaking attempt to repair this critical blood vessel. The surgeons also needed to realign the patient's thighbone and then stabilize it by inserting long pins through one side of the outer leg, through the femur, and then out through the other side of the leg. Throughout this long surgery, I manually breathed for him using the field anesthesia equipment.

After his surgery was completed, I transported him to the ICU. Shortly after arriving in the ICU the patient began to exhibit brady-cardia (slow heart rate) and dysrhythmias (irregular heartbeats). I responded immediately when the ICU staff yelled, "Get anesthesia in here!" and I quickly administered atropine followed by epinephrine, emergency drugs used to stimulate the heart's pumping action and prevent the patient's blood pressure from falling. We began cardiopul-monary resuscitation (CPR), and when the anesthesiologist arrived shortly thereafter, he ordered us to stop the CPR efforts. The tremen-dous amount of time and supplies we had invested in this individual and his rapidly deteriorating physical state did not warrant the contin-uation of heroic measures. The patient would be pronounced dead twenty minutes after arriving in the ICU.

The helicopters carrying the wounded would come and go. Some choppers brought in patients while others medevaced those who had been stabilized to another location for further care. We never knew when the choppers would be arriving, so we used the time in between surgeries to clean instruments, equipment, and gear. Preventing our equipment from being destroyed by the dirt being thrown up and into the ORs by the takeoff and landing of the helicopters was a constant struggle.

Conditions within the ORs were less than ideal and anything but sterile. Flies and dirt seemed to find their way onto and into everything. We tried to keep our equipment covered with tarps to prevent small granules of dirt and sand from impregnating and destroying it, but we would eventually lose the use of a few portable ventilators because of this dirt and sand contamination. Instead of having separate suction equipment—one for the surgical procedure itself and one for use by the anesthetist—the same noisy suction machine and equipment were shared by both the surgeons and the anesthesia provider.

Lightbulbs strung across the ceiling provided the lighting in these rooms. These bulbs, powered by generator, would flicker frequently and would periodically die out completely. Many times we would have only our headlamps to illuminate the anesthesia area and the surgical field. Intravenous fluid bags were strung up by ropes to whatever we could find in order to keep them elevated. Because the rooms were erected on dirt floors, clearing the blood that had flowed from the patient and soaked into the ground required nothing more than shoveling it up and pitching it outside the tent.

Although we lacked many surgical instruments and supplies that would normally be used to perform the same surgeries in a stateside hospital, we learned to improvise, devising ways to reuse items and conserve resources. The abdominal pads normally used only once to soak up blood and fluids from wounds were wrung out by the surgeons and reused on the same patient. We had no idea how long we would be at Camp Anderson, nor did we know how many casualties would be brought to us for care. The quantity and availability of supplies and resources were constant worries for us.

That first full night in Camp Anderson, we experienced brief periods when we could rest in between the arrivals of the casualties.

Because no berthing tents had been set up, we simply located a place outside one of the tents where we placed a cot and stowed our personal gear. I chose a spot next to OR number two so that I was readily available for the arrival of any incoming wounded or to relieve Dave Sheppard from a case with which he might be involved.

Friday, 4 April, arrived. The temperature quickly rose to more than one hundred degrees, creating a sweltering, suffocating environment within the ORs. Despite the boiling outside temperature, we kept the OR tent flaps down to prevent flies from coming inside. This caused the operating rooms to become even hotter, but we worked on.

The choppers continued arriving, bringing us more and more wounded. We saw untold gunshot wounds that had resulted in severe, devastating injuries to the head, face, neck, torso, abdomen, arms, and legs. Gaping, bloody holes were torn through every part of the body. Limbs dangled from bodies, held by a slight thread of flesh, or they had been ripped off completely. Faces smeared with a mixture of blood, sweat, and dirt were recognizable as human solely by the piercing eyes looking up in fear and pain. Others were suffering from sucking chest wounds, charred flesh, shattered bones, or partially blown-away skulls—their brain matter was missing, but the individual continued to breathe because the brain stem remained intact. Even small, relatively harmless-looking external bullet holes to the abdomen would reveal extensive internal damage to the bowel, bladder, stomach, liver, and spleen. It was a horrible, gruesome, and heart-wrenching sight.

We received and treated all those who had become a casualty of this war: American fighting men, Iraqi soldiers, and the innocent Iraqi women and children who were at the wrong place at the wrong time. Their screams of excruciating pain filled the air, and the stench of destroyed flesh and death was revolting as it intensified in the sweltering Iraqi heat. I thought I had entered hell when I arrived at Camp Guadalcanal with its primitive conditions. Now I believed I had moved ever deeper into hell, for I had truly entered the hell of war.

As the wounded continued to arrive and the scenes of overwhelming and incomprehensible human devastation and destruction seemed as though they would never cease, I realized we were struggling and doing everything in our power to keep these people alive while others were struggling just as hard to kill them. This was war—a war being fought just as diligently within the canvas tent walls of Bravo Surgical Company's trauma field hospital as it was being fought on the battle-field. The question was, who was really winning?

With the rapid and constant arrival of casualties, we had little time to ponder our thoughts or our feelings. All of our efforts were focused toward saving as many lives as possible with whatever supplies and equipment we had, and despite the less-than-ideal environment in which we were working.

One of my patients was an Iraqi man who had been shot in his abdomen. His colon had been ruptured, and his abdominal cavity was filled with human waste. For some reason I could not maintain adequate oxygen saturation for him despite my constant manual ventilation. A chest tube had been inserted and connected to suction, and there was no evidence that the patient was bleeding from a thoracic injury. Still, I knew something was not right. The patient's oxygen saturation level, which should have been 95 to 100 percent, had fallen to 89 percent. I told Cdr. Mark Fontana, the surgeon who was performing the proce-dure, "The oxygen saturation levels are down to 89 percent. I'm not sure what's wrong. I hear breath sounds bilaterally [indicating that both lungs were being ventilated and receiving oxygen], and I am ventilating him but not oxygenating him. Something's wrong."

A decision to stop the abdominal procedure and open the thoracic area was made. It was a drastic decision, but a necessary one. Once the chest was opened, we saw a tennis ball–sized hole on the upper portion of his right lung, and he was oozing blood. I was ventilating him, but the oxygen was not entering his bloodstream; instead, it was being blown out through this large, gaping hole in his lung. He exhibited no obvious symptoms, such as subacute emphysema, crepitus (crackling, crinkling, or grating feeling or sound around the lungs due to the infiltration of air), or bleeding that would indicate such a significant wound had been sustained.

Once the surgeons saw this devastating, fatal wound, they looked at one another and said, "This surgery is over. We can't help this man anymore."

I looked at Commander Fontana and said, "It's over? What am I supposed to do?"

"You've got to let him die, Cheryl," he said, and began backing away from the table.

The only thing that was keeping this man alive was my effort to ventilate him continuously by squeezing the anesthesia reservoir bag. I was breathing for him, and his life was literally in my hands.

The surgeons stopped the procedure, moved away from the table, and removed their gowns. Still, I could not stop squeezing the bag. This was not something one learns in anesthesia school, and I was not prepared for such a gut-wrenching, decisive, and final act. The OR nurses began cleaning up, and all the surgeons had left, but I still continued squeezing the bag. I could not stop myself despite the continuous decline of this man's oxygen saturation levels. I realized that he was dying, that his brain was being deprived of oxygen, and that nothing more could be done to save his life. Still, I continued to squeeze the bag.

A few of my colleagues entered the OR and said, "Cheryl, the surgeons aren't coming back. We're done; it's over." Still, I continued to squeeze the bag. I needed time to convince myself that I had no choice but to stop this man's life. I was fully in charge of him at that moment, and my action was the only thing sustaining his life.

As I sat there, I experienced a memory flash from a time when I was stationed on board the USNS *Mercy*. We had talked about what we would do if the ship was hit by enemy fire and we had no way of taking our patients to safety before the ship sank. We did not want them to experience the abhorrent death by drowning, so we developed a plan where we would dose the patients with morphine to provide them with a peaceful death before they went down with the ship.

That memory gave me the strength I needed. I administered ten milligrams of morphine to my patient and began to slow the rhythm with which I was squeezing the bag. Eventually and very gradually, I stopped squeezing the bag. My patient was dead. I could only pray that his death was a peaceful one.

I then asked the OR nurse to get Commander Fontana to come back into the OR and officially pronounce the death of this man. When she returned, she said, "Cheryl, the doctors can't come back in right now. It's your call." This task was way beyond the normal scope of duties and responsibilities for a nurse anesthetist, but we were not functioning in normal times. I pronounced his death, and as I completed my anesthesia record I wondered who, if anyone, would ever read it. I was emotionally exhausted and physically spent.

When Iraqi civilians or EPWs died or arrived at the camp dead on arrival, we would take whatever identification we could find on them and send it to the Iraqi government. Their remains were taken to a trench on the far side of the road that bordered the camp. They were then placed there with deep respect in accordance with their religious customs. The precise location of their remains was recorded using the global positioning system, and that location was reported to the Iraqi government. Following the demise of my patient, I could do nothing more than watch as the corpsmen gently and respectfully removed this man from the OR and took him to his final resting place, the trench on the other side of the road.

Despite the heart-wrenching experience I had just endured, my work was far from complete. More casualties arrived, and we soon realized that this war was not one in which only the fighting troops were being killed and injured. A nine-year-old boy arrived with half of his face blown off. Where he once sported a nose was now nothing more than shredded tissue. His right eye was gone, as was most of the right side of his face. He was in excruciating pain, had only half a mouth, yet he cried, screamed, and called out for his mother. Even though he spoke a different language from our own, the cry for "Mom" was universal. We knew what he wanted and what he needed, and we did everything we could to comfort him.

I saw this young boy in the triage area, where he was being evaluated by anesthesia because of his seriously impaired airway. We had little pediatric equipment on our Authorized Minimum Medical Allowance List (AMMAL) because children are not considered to be frequent victims of war. Fortunately, a small endotracheal tube was located, and Capt. James Chimiak, an anesthesiologist, expertly inserted it with his skilled hands. The vision of that helpless, innocent, mangled child still haunts me and will remain with me forever in my dreams and in my nightmares.

I had never been exposed to such an overwhelming degree of human destruction or been a witness to such terrible, horrific wounds. What I was witnessing was far beyond the accident victims and single-gunshot-wound casualties I had cared for in my past. The sights we witnessed were haunting, and the smells of this hell invaded our senses and penetrated deep into our very souls.

For forty-six hours we continued to care for incoming casualties, many of whom required surgery. During that period OR number one performed ten complicated and extensive surgeries on two EPWs and eight marines. Those of us assigned to OR number two performed fifteen surgeries on fourteen EPWs and one marine. Because our U.S. Marines were equipped with armored vests, many of them were spared being wounded severely in the chest and abdomen; instead, most of their wounds were to the arms, legs, and lower torso. As a result, more marines were operated on in OR number one, where their orthopedic wounds were surgically repaired. They would then be medevaced to the EMF.

All the surgical cases for which I provided anesthesia care in OR number two, whether Iraqi civilian, EPW, or marine, were memorable ones. Still, one marine who was brought into our OR after he had sustained a gunshot wound to the neck would prove to be one of the most unforgettable and emotional cases I would experience throughout my entire twenty-five-year career in the navy.

That young marine's name was Jeff.

# 16

## CARING FOR JEFF

Jeff was brought to Camp Anderson in a helicopter after sustaining a wound to his neck. He was swiftly removed from the chopper and carried to the triage tent on a litter. Prompt evaluation of his wounds revealed the need to establish an airway as quickly as possible because his trachea was already moved off center.

Jeff was awake and alert when he was placed on our table in OR number two. His sparkling blue eyes were filled with pain and fear as he looked up at me. The wound he had sustained was severe, and he was gasping for breath. A hematoma (a mass of clotted blood) had formed around his carotid artery, causing pressure against his trachea and deviating it. He was able to breathe, but the deviation of his trachea was so severe that endotracheal intubation, or the insertion of a tube into his mouth and down into the trachea to provide an open airway for the administration of oxygen and anesthetic, would be difficult if not impossible.

Prior to Jeff's arrival, we had received a brief report of his condition from the triage personnel and were prepared to perform a tracheotomy, an emergency procedure requiring the surgical formation of an opening into the trachea through the neck to allow the passage of air. Commander Fontana, the surgeon in the case, said, "Cheryl, we are getting an airway casualty in, and I plan to trach him (perform a tracheotomy) if you cannot get a tube in."

Jeff was scared, and his fear was intoxicating. He had been informed in the triage area that a tracheotomy might be needed to save his life. I introduced myself and told him, "Jeff, I'm going to put a mask over your face to give you oxygen. I'm going to take real good care of you."

As soon as I began to cover his nose and mouth with the oxygen mask, he said, "Hold it. Please, please don't cut my throat." Having been informed by one of the physicians in the triage area that a tracheotomy might be needed, he fully understood what might occur, and he was begging me to stop the surgeons from performing that procedure. As I looked into his eyes, I could readily see the fear and anguish on his face, and I felt his fear deep within my soul. I said, "Jeff, I am going to do everything I can to get this airway into you. Just know that I am going to take the best care of you that I can." It was now totally up to me to do all I could to grant his wish of not having the surgeons cut his throat.

Despite years of training, to a certified nurse anesthetist, a patient with a difficult airway is the most humbling and challenging endeavor that our specialty encounters. Unlike a stateside hospital that is well lighted and safe and possesses ready access to the most advanced technological equipment and supplies, our wartime OR number two included nothing but the barest of essentials. This was the time, the final reckoning that would answer the two questions that had haunted me throughout my many days of deployment. Did I truly have the knowledge, skill, and expertise needed to provide the best medical care to our wounded troops? Would I find the strength to make the best decision and do the right thing?

After reassuring Jeff, I induced unconsciousness and then administered succinylcholine, a rapid-acting anesthesia agent that produces skeletal muscle paralysis. With this administration, I knew I had crossed the bridge; he was no longer capable of spontaneous breathing. I had to get the endotracheal tube inserted and inserted quickly, or the surgeons would have no choice but to perform the tracheotomy. I closed my eyes and prayed, "God, please help me to do this."

When I looked down into Jeff's throat I could not see an opening, just a mass of soft tissue and blood. Relying on my previous clinical experiences, I knew I needed to arc the endotracheal tube a bit more than usual and scoop upward. I just knew the trachea *had* to be there. God had to be guiding my hand, for when I inserted the tube it miraculously slid down right into his trachea. Jeff now had an established airway in which to administer life-saving oxygen. We would not need to perform a tracheotomy, and his plea "please don't cut my throat" could and would be honored.

I immediately hooked him up to the breathing circuit and began oxygenating him. His chest rose bilaterally, indicating that oxygen was entering both lungs, and the endotracheal tube began to fog with his carbon dioxide exhalation. I never was able to visualize his vocal cords before inserting that tube, but I had no doubt, on the basis of the bilateral rise of his chest and the fogging to the tube, that the tube had been inserted exactly where it was supposed to be. When I looked up at the crew in the OR, they all began cheering. They had been standing back, holding their breaths, watching and praying for my success with the insertion of the tube. Their cheers, combined with the grateful look radiating in their eyes, brought me to tears. All I could do was thank God, for he had definitely come through when I needed him the most. He had answered my prayers and the prayers of all who were a witness to this event.

Because the gunshot had created significant and massive damage so close to the carotid artery (one of two principal vessels supplying blood to the brain), performing surgery under the primitive conditions in which we were surrounded was determined to be too risky. We knew we did not have enough blood should the artery rupture. Jeff could easily bleed to death on the table if such an event occurred.

I steadfastly secured the endotracheal tube and filled syringes with vecuronium (a longer-acting neuromuscular blocking agent), midazolam (used to produce drowsiness and to relieve anxiety), and various narcotics. I sat there continuously squeezing the Ambu bag and breathing for Jeff as we waited for a chopper to land that would take him farther away from enemy lines to a better-equipped, more sophisticated trauma center.

While I waited, I realized I had formed a deep emotional bond with Jeff and did not want to pass his care off to someone who might not understand how miraculous the insertion of this airway had been or how important it was to keep intact. If this endotracheal tube should become dislodged, I believed there would be no way for it to be successfully inserted again, especially if Jeff was on the helicopter when this happened. Even the possibility of performing a tracheotomy with the rapidly developing hematoma was high risk; the most skilled surgeon could easily cut into the hematoma, and Jeff would then bleed to death. I hated the thought of handing over Jeff's care to another and decided I needed to provide him with anything I had that might foster his chances of survival.

Before I left the States, I had taken a Jackson Reese/Mapleson ventilation unit from NMC, Portsmouth, and carried it with me in my Alice pack. This unit had a latex Ambu bag that was more pliable than the hard rubber construction of the bags we routinely used. It allowed easy adjustment to the flow of oxygen, and positive pressure could be applied to it if necessary to keep a patient's alveoli (tiny sacs in the lungs) open. Less than forty-eight hours into caring for the wounded of this war, I had decided to give up my only special ventilation unit to Jeff without really knowing how many other Jeffs I would need to provide care for. Still, something inside me said, "Give this to Jeff. He needs it," so I decided it would be my special gift to him along with several oxygen cylinders I had prepared to accompany him while he was being transported.

A chopper landed, and along with the corpsmen, I accompanied Jeff as four stretcher bearers took him to the helicopter pad. All throughout this transport process to the chopper, I kept breathing for him by rhythmically and steadily compressing the Jackson Reese/ Mapleson bag. The blades of the helicopter continued to rotate, kicking up dust and dirt all around us. Little could be heard over the rumble and roar of those massive rotating blades. Still, as we lifted Jeff up into the chopper, I screamed to the receiving corpsman on board, "Keep squeezing the bag! Keep him alive! Keep him alive!" I had written out on a tiny piece of paper when and how often to give Jeff the syringes of vecuronium and midazolam I had drawn up. I tried to yell over the noise of the rotating blades, for I desperately needed to know that the corpsman on board the chopper understood my orders. He gave me the thumbs-up sign.

Briefly looking over at the pilot who had turned to face me, I could readily see that he was in a rush to take off. He wanted to get this guy in, get him settled, get off the ground, and transport him quickly. For a split second I reviewed in my mind how I had managed to pull off the task of inserting Jeff's airway. It had taken everything in me, and now I had to trust that these guys would also do everything they could for Jeff. I had no other choice but to believe they would, and as I looked at Jeff one last time, I handed over to the corpsman the Jackson Reese/Mapleson bag and begged him again, "Keep squeezing the bag. Keep him alive! Keep him alive!"

Turning Jeff's care over to another was an agonizing and highly emotional experience for me. I had no idea where he was going or whether the corpsman on board the helicopter had heard my plea. All I could do was let him go and pray that he would be okay. I had done everything in my power to honor his wishes and to save his life. It would not be until I returned to Kuwait a month and a half later that I would learn of Jeff's fate.

# 17

## WE ARE "DEVIL DOCS"

W e had been at Camp Anderson for three days, and our mobile tent trauma center had received, evaluated, and treated a total of 106 casualties in the course of forty-six hours. These casualties were a result of fierce frontline fighting between the U.S. Marines and the Iraqi enemy troops. Bravo Surgical Company, along with some of the FRSS and STP units, was the closest medical groups adjacent to the frontline.

Dr. Sanjay Gupta, the CNN reporter we had encountered earlier, was still on hand providing medical news and information about the activities of medical personnel as they applied their skills and expertise in an attempt to save lives and repair the devastating wounds of war. I first noticed both Dr. Gupta and his photographer, "Mad Dog," when we were waiting for transportation at Camp Hasty. Wearing a multi-pocketed vest where various rolls of film and other photographic para-phernalia could easily be stored, and carrying cameras and a tripod, Mad Dog, as all could see, was a civilian. Both Dr. Gupta and Mad Dog were standing with the marines at Camp Hasty, and I was never sure whether they were also waiting for transportation or trying to locate the position of one of our FRSS units.

Commander Fontana and some of the other more senior Bravo Company officers began talking with them. We then learned that both Dr. Gupta and Mad Dog decided to travel with us to Camp Anderson, where they would spend every moment of those three horrific days with us providing live, on-the-scene reports via videophone to CNN viewers stateside.

During one of the first reports that Dr. Gupta broadcasted, the medical personnel of the Bravo Surgical Company were referred to as "Devil Docs." The origin of that moniker dates back to World War I. During the battle of Belleau Wood, the U.S. Marines fought so fiercely against the Germans that the enemy referred to them as *Teufel-hunden,* or "Devil Dogs," a reference to the vicious, wild mountain dogs of Bavarian folklore. Soon afterward, marine recruiting posters depicted a snarling English bulldog wearing a U.S. Marine Corps helmet. The tenacity and demeanor of the Devil Dog depicted in this image took root with both the marines and the public. The marines were proud to adopt this nickname for themselves, and the name Devil Docs was a natural extension applied to the medical personnel who provide care to marines on the battlefield. We, the members of the Bravo Surgical Company, readily embraced this sobriquet, for it was a perfect fit with what we were doing inside the hellhole into which we had entered.

We knew little of the specific content or nature of Dr. Gupta's reports being broadcast to our friends and families in the States, but we respected him and believed his reporting would be factual and just. We knew we were doing everything we possibly could to save lives in extremely brutal conditions and under horrific circumstances. Our hope was that through his reports, our loved ones at home would know where we were and that we were safe and working diligently to repair the wounds of war. Dr. Gupta's news reports had become our only means of conveying information that might allay the fear of those we loved back home.

The respect we had for Dr. Gupta went well beyond his role as a news reporter. He was a skilled surgeon, and as we had noticed earlier, he did not hesitate to assist us in the OR despite the role conflict he experienced with being an objective journalist detached from the story he was covering and actually becoming a participant in that same story. Whenever the need arose for him to switch into the role of surgeon, he was there for us, and we were all very appreciative. The source of his motivation was the same as ours: make the right decision, do the right thing, and perform whatever role was needed to save the lives of others. Not much else really mattered.

Dr. Gupta stuck with us during those tumultuous three days at Camp Anderson and beyond. We developed a close, collegial relationship with him. He was a good guy: modest, warm, gentle, caring, highly skilled, and not afraid to do the right thing even though pundits and others might criticize his decisions and actions. He soon became our friend, and we considered him to be one of us, just another Devil Doc in the sands of Iraq doing all we could to save the casualties of war.

We knew that part of his responsibility in his role as a journalist was the development of one of the "Special Edition of CNN Presents" programs. This program would document the journey and actions of the Bravo Surgical Company during our days in Iraq. I could not fathom how a one-hour video would be able to capture the true essence of all we had experienced at Camp Anderson and would continue to experience for the forty days we would spend in Iraq, but I trusted that he would do us justice.

Dr. Sanjay Gupta was one of us. He was just another member of the Bravo Surgical Company, and he would remain at our side as we packed up and moved forward, ever closer to Baghdad.

# 18

## SURVIVING IN THE WAKE
## OF DEATH

The process of packing up our surgical company began the evening of 5 April. The personnel in OR number one closed early that evening to begin dismantling their tent and equipment so they could be packed in ISO containers. OR number two remained intact, and we continued performing surgery on all casualties as they were brought to Camp Anderson.

Those of us in OR number two worked until 2:30 the following morning. We cared for five patients and performed such surgical procedures as exploratory laparotomies, bowel resections with colostomy (surgically creating an anus by connecting the colon to an opening in the abdominal wall), and the removal of some damaged tissue from a knee that had been shattered by gunshot. We were exhausted as we found our way to our cots located outside the OR tent walls. As I removed my boots, something I had not done for sixty hours, my socks were dripping in sweat, and my feet were raw.

Reveille was sounded at 5 AM, allowing us a brief two and one-half hours of sleep. Because we had no water for washing ourselves, I cleaned up as best I could with hand wipes. We continued to wear the same clothes as those we wore when we began our journey into Iraq on 2 April: green T-shirts, MOPP pants, and underclothes, all of which were stained and encrusted with dried blood, sweat, and what seemed like a ton of dirt. Cleanliness and personal hygiene were not issues; we were all filthy, and we all reeked of old dried sweat and foul body odor, but we knew we could do nothing about it. We also knew we would just become more grubby and soiled as the day wore on.

We immediately began dismantling OR number two, hauling, dragging, pushing, and pulling the equipment and tenting to be stowed in ISO containers. It was strenuous, hard work compounded by physical fatigue, windy hot weather, and sore, battered feet.

By noon the entire camp was packed, and we began the wait for the trucks that would take us to Camp Chesty, forty miles to our north and approximately seventy miles south of Baghdad. Both our mission and our goal were the same: to stay a short distance behind the advancing troops of the 1st MEF in order to continue providing surgical damage control to the wounded.

Despite the danger of traveling through Iraq in a convoy, we had little choice. At least this journey was scheduled for the daylight hours, and we would have more protection from marines armed with M-16s riding with us. One marine was assigned to ride in the back of each truck that was carrying personnel, and one would serve as a driver. This arrangement did not provide a lot of protection, but it was twice as much as we had had when we made our perilous journey from Camp Hasty to Camp Anderson.

Sitting on our Alice packs in the exposed and harsh Iraqi landscape beneath a blazing sun, we waited and waited to board the convoy trucks. Hot, tired, miserable, and filthy, we could do little more than sit there breathing in the stench of the pit that had served as our bathroom and as the place we had burned discarded body parts, human tissue, and bloody rags. We sustained ourselves on small snacks from our MREs, but the heat, combined with the stench, left us with little appetite.

As I sat waiting for the convoy trucks to arrive, I reflected on the past few days since our arrival in Iraq and what we had accomplished at this first temporary hospital. I thought about Jeff and the little nine-year-old boy and wondered where they were and how they were doing. I also wondered what the future would hold for us. How many casualties would we care for? Would we have enough supplies? What would our next camp be like?

The trucks arrived, and we began boarding at 2:30 PM. The convoy comprised thirty vehicles: seven-ton trucks to transport ISO containers and personnel, ambulances, and marine security vehicles that would drive at the front of the convoy. Each of the seven-ton trucks towed a cart behind it, which is where we would stow our Alice packs and our one seabag. We were told that our journey north was expected to take four hours and that we would be going through an area around "the canal," which was infested with enemy snipers. We all wore full MOPP gear, Kevlar vests, and helmets, with our loaded pistols strapped to our sides.

I sat with Dave Sheppard and one of our OB/GYN doctors, Cdr. Ken Singleton, on hard, thin metal benches lining the sides of the truck's bed. Unlike the one in which I had ridden to Camp Anderson, this truck was covered with a canvas canopy, and the interior was sweltering hot and suffocating. Still, at least we were leaving the hellhole of Camp Anderson, and we believed anything could be endured for four hours.

Our convoy journey began at 3:20 PM, and we slowly rumbled our way north. We passed several dead camels lying on the roadside and saw the shattered remains of several bombed-out buildings. Interspersed among the building ruins were flowers, a sight I had not seen in months, and I thought they were beautiful.

Many of the small villages we passed through had been deserted, but others were full of small children trying to sell us cigarettes. We remembered the previous warnings about the children approaching the trucks and about not interacting with them in any way. These children could be nothing more than decoys used to draw us out of the trucks where we would become easy targets for a sniper's bullet.

At 5:15 PM, our convoy stopped abruptly and sat idle on the road. We had not arrived at any particular destination; we simply stopped. As

I sat in the back of the seven-ton truck, I began to hear the sounds of heavy artillery fire and then watched the sky light up from the explosions of rockets and missiles being fired from the ground and from Cobra and Apache aircraft in the sky. The convoy we had been closely following was being ambushed by enemy troops.

We could not advance, and we could not go back. All we could do was sit and wonder whether the truck in which we were riding would be the next to be attacked. We were in the middle of a battlefield and had no place to go. We were sitting targets. The walls of the truck, the M-16 rifles carried by the small contingent of marines riding with us, and our own small-caliber pistols were our only protection. Some of the marines had jumped off the trucks and lay prone on the road's embankment with their rifles aimed and ready to fire at anyone approaching the convoy. Cobra and Apache helicopters flew over our heads searching for any movement of enemy troops advancing toward us.

We sat, and we sat, and we sat. We had no water or food. Our Alice packs and canteens were stowed in the trailer being pulled behind the truck. To access them would require leaving the truck and exposing ourselves to enemy fire. Attired in full MOPP gear with helmets on, we were stifling hot and sweating profusely. Our butts were numb from sitting on the metal seats, and our backs were aching from the prolonged cramped sitting position in which we were forced to remain. Any attempt to stand up in the truck would do little more than cause a bulge in the canvas roof and form a ready target for enemy fire. Answering the "call of nature" was not a concern. We were too dehydrated, and what little fluid we had left in our systems was being rapidly excreted in the form of sweat. There were many moments when I thought that being killed would be less painful than continuing to endure the misery of sitting in that truck.

As if he were reading my mind, Dave turned to me and said, "Cheryl, do you have anything you need to say to anybody?"

"What do you mean?" I asked.

"Have you said everything you wanted to say to everyone you ever wanted to say it to?" he clarified.

I thought for a moment and said, "Yeah, I have."

"Good," he responded. "Because we might die tonight, do you know that?" Pausing briefly, he then asked, "Did you have a good life?"

It took but a moment to respond. I looked at him, smiled, and said, "You know what, Dave? I did have a good life." I felt those words resonate deep within my soul. They spoke a truth that reflected the very essence of my being, and I was enveloped in a sense of peace.

As I thought about the question Dave asked me, I realized it was similar to what I had asked Kathy just before she died. I had no idea when I asked her that question sixteen months earlier that it would also be posed to me while I sat in a convoy truck somewhere in Iraq. It was eerie.

Dave and I continued talking about our lives and the real possibility that, at the age of forty-five, our lives could quickly end with a single shot from a sniper's rifle. It could happen in the next minute or in the next hour; we just did not know. Our conversation was not a morbid one, and talking openly about our own deaths did not cause us pain or fear.

As we sat listening to the sound of nearby mortar and rifle fire, both fully aware that we were in the midst of battle, we talked and reflected on the course of our lives. Had I done everything in my life that I wanted to do? Had I said everything I wanted to say to others? Had I made good decisions and tried to do the right thing? Could I die now and have no regrets? Yes, yes, yes, and yes!

These insights and revelations gave me a keen sense of power and control. I may have been in a very vulnerable, life-threatening situation, but I did not feel vulnerable, and I was not afraid for my own life. My concern continued to be for those who would survive me: my sister, my mother, my family, and my friends. Still, I was comforted knowing that I had done everything I could to make it as easy as possible for those who would be required to settle my affairs.

Reveling in that peaceful feeling, I began to daydream. Beautiful, serene, and simple images appeared in my mind's eye with acute clarity. Without even thinking, I said, "God, I would love a piece of *cold* watermelon right now."

Ken Singleton smiled at me as he said, "When my wife and I were on our honeymoon, we had this wonderful sherbet made from fresh pineapple. It was so cold and delicious."

As he continued to describe this delectable treat, I could see it as clearly as if it was right in front of me, and I could even feel the coolness radiating from it. There it was, nestled in a stainless steel cup that was beaded with condensation. I could even see the gentle wisp of cool vapor rising from its domed surface. I had never experienced anything like this before; it was so surreal, and yet at the same time it was very, very real!

It seemed Ken, Dave, and I were all seeing this same delicious, cool, incredible image floating right before us, just out of reach. Our mouths were watering, and we were all licking our lips, wanting so badly to taste the cold, wet, sweet essence of this cup of pineapple sherbet.

Tearing our eyes away from this delightful shared aberration, we looked at one another. With our mouths twisted and our faces askew, trying to control the drool and saliva that had been produced by this image, we looked so comical that all three of us burst out laughing. God, it felt so good to laugh and to feel such a refreshing sense of joy. It was probably even better and more satisfying than savoring the cold, sweet taste of the sherbet that had been there one moment and was gone the next.

Those traveling in the truck with us had little appreciation of what Dave, Ken, and I had experienced. The sound of our hearty, uncontrollable laughter was met with groans, mumbles, curses, and comments to "shut up." Our traveling companions were scared and could find very little humor in the situation that surrounded us. To them, we may have appeared to be insane or were just being silly, making light of our precarious, volatile, and potentially deadly situation. We did everything we could to stifle our laughter, for we respected them and did not want to be just another irritant in the cramped, uncomfortable space in which we were confined.

The convoy remained stationary for a total of five long, miserable hours. Gradually the sounds of gunfire subsided and then stopped completely. It was close to 10:30 PM when the truck engines were started and the tires began to roll slowly forward. It was pitch-black outside, and we could see very little as we continued our slow, monotonous progression north. Three more hours would elapse before we finally arrived safely at Camp Chesty, where we were cordially greeted with the directive to "sleep wherever you can find a spot."

# 19

# CAMP CHESTY

Although our welcome to Camp Chesty was terse, indifferent, and somewhat insensitive, we took no offense. We were in a war zone and were too exhausted, dehydrated, and physically and emotionally spent to take much notice. All we wanted was to get out of those damn trucks, retrieve our gear from the trailers, drink voraciously from whatever water source we could access, and find that "spot" where we could lie down and sleep. We did not need to be directed to the "bathroom facilities." We still had no urge to relieve ourselves. I would go a total of twelve full hours before experiencing the urge or need to urinate.

Some of my battle buddies chose to find their sleeping spot in or on the trucks. I chose a spot on the ground in between two of the seven-ton trucks. I wedged myself alongside one of the truck's tires and lay down in full gear with my helmet on. Once again, my pistol, ready to fire, was within easy reach at my side.

We started the morning of 7 April at 5:30. I realized as I was getting up off the ground from my sleeping spot that I had had barely six hours of sleep during the last forty-eight hours. We were all tired. Our

150

bodies were stiff and sore from sitting so many interminable hours in the trucks and from sleeping on the cold ground. The brief three hours of sleep we were able to get since arriving at Camp Chesty had provided little relief to our weary bodies.

Camp Chesty, named in honor of Gen. Lewis B. "Chesty" Puller of the U.S. Marines, incorporated a very large area of land approximately seventy miles south of Baghdad. It included an airstrip, and unlike the simple road on which we had landed when we first arrived in Iraq, this runway was actually built for the takeoff and landing of aircraft. The U.S.–led coalition ground forces had taken this area over from the Iraqis and secured it for use by our military. The runway even had some hardened fixed hangars on both ends of the strip that had once served as shelter for Iraqi aircraft. These were now being used to house and protect American aircraft from the unrelenting wind, blowing sand, and extreme heat.

We had been deposited on the extreme outer edge within this city-sized camp the night of our arrival, so we were instructed to reload our gear and ourselves back onto the trucks so we could move to a better area inside the camp. The area designated for use by the Bravo Surgical Company was still several more miles within the camp's perimeter.

As we rode through Camp Chesty, we could see that numerous other units, commands, companies, battalions, platoons, and military groups were set up. Instead of being the only military company (and totally isolated, at that), as had been the case at Camps Hasty and Anderson, we would share this camp. Our new neighbors were Seabees, transportation and supply companies, a marine air wing, engineer support battalions, and many other army, navy, marine, and air force military support groups, including several of our medical STPs and a few FRSS units.

All of the various subcamps flew flags designating their company, platoon, unit, or battalion. Soldiers, sailors, marines, and air force personnel were milling about as they prepared to start their day. Camp Chesty was the largest supply depot in the northernmost section of central Iraq and would provide supplies to the frontline troops. In this same compound, but separated from other areas by a ten-foot-high sand berm, was the home of seven thousand Camp Lejeune–based marines of Task Force Tarawa.

After arriving at our designated area within this tent city, we jumped down from the trucks and immediately began setting up the tents and facilities of our surgical support company. In addition to erecting our triage unit, ORs, ICU, and ward, we would set up berthing tents so we would no longer need to sleep out in the open, shielded by nothing more than black skies and twinkling stars. We had arrived at the place that would serve as our home until we were once again ordered to move on.

Battling the strong winds that only increased as the day wore on, we pushed and we pulled, dislodging, lifting, and carrying the heavy items stored within the ISO containers. The wind pummeled the canvas of our tents, and we struggled to raise and secure them onto their dirt-and-grit foundations. This brutal and strenuous labor continued to wreak havoc on our tired, battered bodies. A light rain began to fall in the afternoon, causing brown streaks to appear on us as the water flowed down our dirt-encrusted faces and arms.

Once the tents were set up, the equipment and supplies were secured, and the ISO containers were emptied, we received our berthing assignments. Fortunately, one of the FRSS units was set up and ready. That unit would be responsible for performing any surgical procedures on casualties arriving during the night; we had been temporarily relieved of our surgical duties. All we needed to do was locate our assigned berthing area and prepare for what we longed for most, a good night's sleep that would repair and mend our exhausted bodies, rest our minds, and fortify our souls.

Berthing assignments for the female officers were made according to work groups so that only those who were required to assist at a surgical procedure or care for an incoming wounded casualty would be awakened. I was assigned with nine others to an old general-purpose tent that was a wobbly, rectangular canvas shell erected on a dirt floor. Constructed of heavy canvas, this tent would tilt precariously on its fragile pole framing and cave in completely when the wind blew too hard. Improving its stability required many hours of work filling sandbags, placing them two to three layers high around the tent's base, and pounding more stakes into the ground.

The tent's interior was dark and dank, and the only ventilation was whatever air seeped in through the flaps covering the two small openings that served as its doors. There were no windows. Rolling up an entire side of the tent was the only means by which we could improve ventilation and get more air inside. We quickly realized that raising the sides of the tent was not a reasonable or smart thing to do because it would allow the wind to deliver more dirt inside and invite scorpions to set up residence in our boots or in our sleeping bags. We had no electricity when we first arrived, and once the sun set, we were totally dependent on our flashlights when inside the tent. By contrast, when the moon was out, it was so bright outside that flashlights were not needed.

I claimed a sleeping area at the side of the tent next to one of the entryways. From my sleeping bag, I could look out of the tent and see the helicopters land. When they landed, I would get up to check to see whether they were bringing in wounded or picking them up to transport them to EMFs. If they were bringing them in, I would immediately head over to the OR and begin preparing for the administration of anesthesia.

Water, a scarce commodity, was strictly rationed. A water buffalo, or "bull" (a large water tank that is filled in the rear and then brought to the troops in the front), was available to us when we first arrived, and the most appropriate use of its valuable and sacred content was debated. Whereas some wanted to use the water to drink, others wanted it for washing clothes. We finally decided to use the water contained in that first water buffalo to wash equipment and clean surgical instruments. If any water remained after completing this number-one priority, we would use it for drinking despite the strong smell and taste of bleach used to make it potable. Washing our clothes, hair, and bodies would have to wait; we would continue to clean ourselves the best we could with premoistened towelettes for a few more days.

We had long ago consumed the nine MREs we were issued prior to moving into Iraq. We were now issued two MRE packets a day, and it was up to us how and when we chose to eat them or what to do with them. The meals were contained in small brown cardboard packets measuring approximately eight by five inches; instructions and guidance for consumption were written on the outside of the cardboard container. These statements, written in bold black lettering, said, "Military Rations Are Good Performance Meals," and "In the field you NEED three meals per day." We were issued only two meals a day, so how could we possibly eat three of them?

Additional tips for MRE consumption included: "Eat some of each component to get a balance of nutrients"; "Eat the high carbohydrate items first (crackers, beverage base, fruit, jelly)"; and "Save unopened dry snack items to eat when you are on the move." Some packets also specified vitamins and minerals that had been added and recommended that we should always eat "beverage base, cocoa beverage, cheese spread, Jalapeño cheese spread, peanut butter, crackers, oatmeal cookie bars, chocolate covered cookies, and fruit." As much as we appreciated this guidance and the recommendations printed on the MRE packets, we ate what we liked and traded or gave away the remainder of our rejected items to our battle buddies. Being the conservationists and scavengers that we had become, we also saved the cardboard packing containers, cutting them out carefully so they could be used as postcards to send greetings and well wishes to our friends and families back home.

The contents of the MREs would continue to be our only source of sustenance for almost a full week. Our first hot meal, delivered by marine ground support personnel, was MRE food that had been heated and placed in large serving containers. That first meal of beef stew, rice, cake, and sweet tea was delicious, as were the breakfast meals and other evening meals that eventually were delivered on a regular basis. Our afternoon meal was whatever we chose to eat from our MRE box.

We had neither tables nor chairs on which to sit, but that mattered little to us. We had become masters at sitting, sleeping, and living in dirt, and we even started to look like dirt. We all sported a dingy gray appearance. Our clothes were dirty dirty, our skin was covered with grit, and our teeth, which once sparkled white when we smiled, were now the same shade of gray/brownish tan of our skin and clothing. We all smelled bad.

Initially, our bathroom facility was nothing more than a hole we would dig in the ground and then cover with dirt after we relieved ourselves. A few days after we arrived at Camp Chesty, the Seabees came to our area and built us a "restroom facility." This simple enclosed structure provided a modest semblance of privacy but little else. The toilet seat was nothing but a wooden plank with a hole cut into it. Underneath the hole were barrels to collect our waste. The canvas curtain door would often blow into your face as you sat on the wooden plank or would blow outward, allowing exposure. Visits to these facilities were quick, lest we be overwhelmed by the repugnant and nauseous smells or the hundreds of flies living inside.

We were at the camp for a total of ten full days before a shower or adequate water for bathing was available. The shower was another primitive structure, featuring ice-cold water that would be made available two hours a day for the females and two hours a day for the males. Because of my inability to tolerate cold, I chose not to use the shower facility and instead scrubbed myself using water I poured into a seven-quart Tupperware bowl that I had carried with me from Portsmouth, Virginia. It mattered little whether we washed ourselves in the shower or chose the "GI bath" method of bathing because within five minutes of completing our shower or bath, we would once again be covered with sand and dirt blown by the wind or the swirling blades of the helicopters.

As water buffaloes began to be delivered to us daily, we were permitted to wash out some of our clothes with the surplus water. I used the same Tupperware bowl to hand wash my clothes, all of which were filthy. To dry them, we would drape or hang our various articles of clothing on the tent, where the windswept dirt and sand quickly covered them, causing muddy clumps and stains. Once the clothes were dry, we would simply shake them out and put them on. At least they were a little cleaner than they were before, and some of the rancid odor embedded within the fibers had been purged. Being able to change my ten-day-old underclothes from dirty dirty to clean dirty was wonderful!

By early morning on the second day after our arrival at Camp Chesty, both OR number one and OR number two were set up and ready to receive patients. Once again, both ORs were austere. Each featured a dirt floor, two OR tables placed head-to-head, and poor lighting. Neither room had air-conditioning for several days. With the temperature often reaching 110 degrees during the day, we would open the tent flaps when we were not performing surgery just to let in some air and diminish the stifling heat of the interior. Unfortunately, when we opened the flaps, we could not prevent flies, bees, and mites from entering. Although we tried to keep the OR environment as clean as possible, flies were everywhere, buzzing over surgical fields and open wounds. All our patients received hefty doses of antibiotics.

One of the first patients received for surgery in OR number one was an EPW whose name was General Hussein. He was a cousin of Saddam Hussein, and he had been shot in his right arm. Among his personal belongings was money equivalent to $45,000 in U.S. currency. His resemblance to his cousin was uncanny; he sported the same short dark hair, heavy eyebrows, bushy mustache, and dark eyes. We also could not help but notice and be astounded by the condition of his feet. Whereas our feet were filthy, bloody, and full of calluses and blisters, General Hussein's feet were clean, smooth, and blemish free. They typified the easy, complacent, and luxurious life in which he must have been living prior to the war. As was the case for all EPWs, a marine guard carrying an M-16 was assigned to the general, and he was shackled to his cot when he was taken to the recovery ward.

I received my first case in OR number two at five o'clock that evening. He was an EPW who had sustained severe injuries to his right foot, lower abdomen, right arm, and buttocks. His surgical repair required a right-foot amputation, the debridement and irrigation of the right arm and buttocks, and a bowel resection and colostomy. Because we did not have commercially manufactured colostomy bags, we taped an empty IV bag to his lower outer abdomen to serve as a collection reservoir for bowel contents. The complicated and intense surgery lasted three hours. After removing his breathing tube, I transferred him to the ICU, where he continued recovering. He would survive his wounds.

I returned to my berthing tent at 8 PM and had barely fallen asleep when choppers arrived, bringing in more casualties. The crew of OR number one, having had an opportunity to rest, were up and readily agreed to take whatever surgical cases came in. They would work until two o'clock the following morning caring for five patients, including a marine who had sustained severe head trauma as a result of shrapnel ripping through his helmet. Neurosurgeon and CNN correspondent Dr. Sanjay Gupta opened the marine's skull and removed bone and shrapnel fragments. He then placed an empty IV bag over the area, in effect creating a window because the transparent quality of the plastic bag allowed the doctors and nurses to see the operative site and closely monitor it for potential bleeding, swelling, or infection. It was absolutely amazing and nothing like anything we had ever seen before.

During the first eight days in Camp Chesty, the flow of incoming wounded remained steady but not overwhelming. In addition to Bravo Company's two operating rooms, an FRSS unit was set up and was actively performing surgical procedures. Periodically, the staff of both OR number one and OR number two were given a day off, and the eight-person team of the FRSS unit would assume the duty, taking any surgical cases that were brought in. Still, we remained on standby in the event that more cases than they could adequately handle arrived.

The wounds we saw and the stories of how the injuries occurred were horrific. We provided care to our wounded marines, EPWs, and noncombatant civilians, never turning anyone away and providing the same standard of care for all. Injuries sustained by our fighting coalition forces were generally orthopedic in nature, and we performed many fasciotomies (surgically incising and dividing the fascia or deep tissue) to remove bullets or multiple shards of embedded shrapnel. In addition, if someone suffered multiple bone fractures as a result of being struck by these projectiles, he would need to have open reduction (surgically exposing the bone and realigning the bone structures) and external fixation (stabilizing the bone alignment by inserting long steel pins through one outer side of the affected arm or leg, through the fractured bone, and then out to the other side of the limb). Many of the fractures we saw may have benefited from internal placement of screws, rods, plates, or other prostheses to immobilize the bone during healing, but we were not equipped with these more modern orthopedic hardware devices routinely used in stateside hospitals.

One such marine was brought to us for emergency surgery, having been shot in the arm by an Iraqi sniper. After he was wounded, his battle buddies immediately fired back, and the sniper was shot through the head, killing him instantly. The buddies in the marine's unit diligently sought out the body of the dead sniper and retrieved his identification. We also saved the bullet extracted from the wounded marine's arm, and both "war trophy" items were presented to him. The pieces were well received and seemed to mean a lot to him.

The exhibition of bravery, camaraderie, and loyalty the marines shared with their buddies was extraordinary. A thirty-five-year-old marine sergeant named James was brought to OR number two with shrapnel embedded and dispersed throughout his abdomen and arm. He, along with five of his fellow marines, had been attempting to safely detonate a rocket-propelled grenade. The grenade exploded prematurely, killing two of the marines instantly and fatally wounding another, who died in the chopper en route. The remaining three, all severely wounded, were brought to us.

James was conscious when he was placed on the OR table. Just as I was placing the mask over his face, more helicopters began to land. Hearing the sound of the approaching choppers, he looked up at me and said, "I'm okay. If someone else is worse, take him first." Emotionally moved by his remark, I explained to him that we would assess him thoroughly, as well as the arriving wounded, and that we would take good care of everyone.

Just before the anesthesia took effect and he fell asleep, James looked up at me and said, "Commander, I have three sons at home who expect me to come home and to play hockey with them." I promised him that we would all do our best. The surgery was extensive and would take six and one-half hours to perform, but he would pull through. I thought about his homecoming and the joy his sons would experience being reunited with him. They may be too young to understand all that their dad sacrificed, but he is a true hero in my book.

Several noncombatant foreign nationals (civilians) were brought to us for care. They had severe traumatic shrapnel wounds from exploding ordnance or bullet wounds sustained from being caught in crossfire. Some we could help, but others were just too severely injured. An Iraqi mother was brought in after her ten-year-old son had found a live grenade and brought it into his home. When the mother attempted to take it away, it exploded, decapitating the boy and blowing off half of the mother's skull. Although in the field she had had a tube inserted in the trachea, by the time she arrived at Camp Chesty, she was already demonstrating signs of imminent certain death. Another family of four had been brought in after sustaining injuries when they tried to run through a marine barricade. They all survived, including the four-year-old girl who had shrapnel embedded in her skull.

One day a middle-aged Iraqi man was brought into OR number two after having sustained a significant injury to his arm from a blast. We were told that he, along with two other foreign nationals, had attempted to run through a marine barricade. The other two men riding in the vehicle with him had been killed instantly. As we prepared this man for surgery, he told me he was a civilian pharmacist. I was amazed at how well he could both speak and comprehend the English language. He was well educated, and he discussed with me the actions, indications, and compound structure of various medications I was administering to him. I did not question his story or his alleged status as an Iraqi civilian pharmacist, for he seemed well versed when it came to pharmaceuticals. Still, I found it curious that someone who seemed to understand English to the degree he did would choose not to heed the marines' command to stop when approaching the barricade.

After I had administered anesthesia to him and while the surgery was taking place, other members of our company inventoried his clothing and personal effects. When they found his identification, they were shocked, as was I. He was a three-star general in the Iraqi Republican Guard. I no longer viewed this person whom I was breathing for as a fellow health care "civilian" provider. He had lied, and we realized that we could not be as trusting of those coming to us for care as we wanted to be and that we needed to keep our guard up.

Initially I thought, "How dare this man lie to us?" and it made me angry. Still, I knew I could not allow my feelings to overtake my duty and responsibility to render the best care I was capable of providing. I put my emotions aside and continued to provide him with the same professional standard of care afforded to all who were brought into OR number two. The general survived the surgery, and because of the change in his status from foreign national to EPW, he was transferred to the recovery ward and, like the other EPWs, shackled to his cot and watched by a marine armed with an M-16 rifle.

Our feelings of resentment toward the EPWs for whom we provided care grew as we witnessed the horrible, devastating wounds and injuries sustained by our young American fighting troops. As health care providers and human beings, we fought to curtail these feelings of resentment and hate. Despite this tumultuous emotional battle that raged deep within us, the care we provided to the patients who were brought to us would continue to be equitable for all.

We did make a few logistical modifications in care provision to diminish tensions between our troops and the EPWs for whom we provided care. At no time, whether they were in a chopper, the OR, or the postoperative ward, were the Americans and EPWs housed together. To prevent cross contamination of potential infectious diseases inherent in the various cultures, we separated the anesthesia equipment we used and designated the items either "EPW" or "American." We never used the same anesthesia equipment on EPWs that we used on our American troops.

As the days continued to pass at Camp Chesty, the number of helicopters bringing in wounded became fewer and fewer. We even found ourselves experiencing a three-day period when no surgical procedures would be required. Our company's mission began moving away from surgical treatment to caring for more medical and humanitarian cases for the foreign nationals. Because we were a surgical company equipped to deal with surgical trauma and not medical issues, we could do little to care for some people, such as the child with leukemia who was brought to us by his parents. We also began medically treating some of our own surgical company members suffering from gastroenteritis and other ailments associated with prolonged living in less-than-sanitary conditions.

Bravo Company continued to care for a total of 667 patients, 63 of whom required more than one hundred intricate and convoluted surgical procedures. The injuries were traumatic, bloody, and debilitating, but no member of the U.S. armed forces brought into the ORs for surgery died. They all survived and were transferred to an EMF.

We had worked long and hard and were pleased with our success rate. We were also proud that we had the opportunity to be working in the service of our country and especially proud that we were able to save the lives of so many of our brave American fighting men.

# 20

# "NESTING" IN CAMP CHESTY

Life in Camp Chesty was far from paradise, but every day brought positive changes and improvements to our living conditions. Despite the unpleasantness we experienced visiting the rustic, fly-infested "bathroom" stalls, these stalls were better than running out into the desert to empty our bladder and bowels into a hurriedly dug shallow hole. Water, though constantly rationed, was available for washing our bodies and our clothes and for quenching our thirst. We had shelter, and even though it required constant reinforcement so that it would remain upright, at least it was there, sheltering us from whatever unexpected surprise Mother Nature had in store. Breakfast and dinner meals were hot, and now that our seabags had been delivered, we had access to a few additional personal and much-needed items. We were safe, and life was good, especially in comparison to the chaotic, tumultuous world we had experienced at Camp Anderson.

We had no idea how long we would be at Camp Chesty. It could be a matter of days, or it could be months. Everything depended on the expediency and success of our fighting forces in accomplishing their mission to take control of and liberate Baghdad. Considering the on-again, off-again departure we had experienced when we left Kuwait, and the unreliable and chaotic transportation system inherent with war, we figured we would be staying for a while.

One morning we attended an officers' call and were informed that the U.S. Marine Corps wanted surgical teams established and maintained in three areas: Camp Coyote (northern Kuwait), Camp Viper, and Camp Chesty. We were told we might remain at Camp Chesty for up to three months. I hoped that if we were required to stay in the combat theater of this war, we would remain at Camp Chesty, where we were gradually making improvements and growing accustomed to our living conditions. With fewer surgeries and more free time available, we had started to focus our attention and efforts on "nesting" and making our austere environment as pleasant and as tolerable as possible.

Outside the male officers' berthing tents and close to the ORs, we built a crude, but homey, patio that we referred to as "the OR pad," or simply "the porch." It was a perfect gathering place for OR personnel because we could easily see any injured being brought in and could be at our assigned OR stations within seconds.

We put up some camouflaged web netting to serve as a roof adjacent to one of the tents. Several guys who had carried portable collapsible camp chairs on their backs along with all their other gear set these chairs up and designated them for community use. Whoever dropped by the porch was always welcome to occupy one of the chairs, relax, chat, read magazines and books, or do most anything that person desired.

As seasoned scavengers, we easily located some old boards left behind by the Iraqis and made additional stools and a coffee table. I built the coffee table by filling sandbags, stacking them about four bags high on each side, and placing a large board across these sandbag foundations. The coffee table became the centerpiece of this "pad," where magazines, books, and even personal letters and photos from home were placed to be shared with visitors.

Much of my downtime was spent under the shelter of the porch. The berthing tents were extremely hot and stifling during the day, and our makeshift open-air patio was a much more comfortable and inviting place to sit, read, write letters, socialize, and simply unwind. If any of the OR folks needed to be located quickly, the pad was the place to go because most of us were there when we were not sleeping, running, exercising, or working in the OR.

Our incoming mail had not caught up with us when we first arrived, but it gradually began to filter in. Most of the letters I received had been written well over a month prior. It amazed me how many people back home, whether they knew me or not, truly cared about my well-being. Their words inspired me to take pen in hand and write back, thanking them for their words of support and encouragement and for their thoughtfulness in sending small packages of essential as well as fun items. I cherished every letter and package I received.

Our flimsy general-purpose berthing tent had become well fortified after countless hours devoted to driving stakes, tightening ropes, and placing sandbags around its perimeter. This tent was nothing more than a hot and dirty shelter that housed our belongings and served as a place to sleep, but it was still our home. We had been issued cots on which to sleep, and the installation of electricity that allowed two lightbulbs to be strung across the top of the tent's interior was a welcome addition to our humble abode. We were now able to accomplish a few menial tasks after the sun set, including locating our cot and lying on it without tripping over some article or object that had gone adrift. Adapting to the eccentricities of one another took time, patience, and understanding, but, in general, on most days we all got along well.

A small exchange had been set up within the camp's perimeter. This store, about a thirty-minute walk from Bravo Company's location, offered us an opportunity to purchase such items as junk food (Pringles, cookies, small jars of salsa), flashlights, batteries, soap, cigarettes, chewing tobacco, stationery, green T-shirts, white socks, lip balm, gauze pads, and other small items. The brand and variety of these commodities were limited; you either chose Dial soap or no soap at all. Periodically, the exchange would receive a supply of soda or bottled Gatorade, both of which would sell out quickly. If you were fortunate enough to be in proximity to the exchange, or if you received advance word that a delivery of this cherished commodity was coming in, you might be lucky enough to purchase the strictly enforced limited supply of two sodas per person. Soda, no matter what brand or flavor, with or without caffeine, was a delectable, awesome treat that was so much better tasting than the bleach-treated water we obtained from the water bull. Despite our diligent efforts to make our daily ration of "bull water" more palatable by adding Kool-Aid or other powdered artificial flavoring, it always seemed to taste and smell like bleach.

I had established a comfortable daily routine. An early riser, I would usually meet up with Lt. Cdr. Tom Leonard, an OR nurse, at the OR pad, where we would heat up water for coffee. Tom had a small propane cylinder torch apparatus that he would light and set under a metal cup. Once the water was heated, we would mix it with the instant coffee from one of the MRE packs, and then we would sit back in one of the chairs on the porch, sip our coffee, and greet others as they awoke and joined us. Some of my friends had laughed at me when we were in Camp Guadalcanal because I was constantly picking up and saving single-serving coffee packets I found lying alongside the road or in the trash. Now, as they ventured over to the porch, they would humbly ask me for one of these scavenged packets so they, too, could enjoy a hot cup of coffee to start their day.

Following morning coffee, we would walk over to one of the ORs for morning muster, where Captain Chimiak would pass along information, and we would be notified of our duty assignments. Once muster concluded, I would return to my tent, put on my running gear, and after signing out in the administration tent, begin to run my usual path down the road. I never deviated from the same path, so the OR crew always knew where to find me if I was needed for a surgical case.

Because I always ran the same path at about the same time each day, I would pass many of the same people from different units either running or milling about outside their tents. We would wave or greet one another, and I soon came to think of them as my neighbors, just as I thought of those I would routinely see when I ran in my own neighborhood in the States.

Following my run I would return to my berthing tent, wash up using my Tupperware bowl, and then change my clothes. I would then wash the clothes I wore to run in and hang them outside on the tent to dry. After straightening up my berthing area, I would walk over to the OR to ensure that the equipment and supplies were ready to go for any injured person who might be brought in. Because we were always ready to go, this task took but a few minutes and entailed little more than cleaning away some dust, checking cylinders, and ensuring that the anesthesia machine was functioning properly.

The remainder of the morning would be spent maintaining the tents by pounding a few stakes or refilling sandbags if we noticed some of the sand had spilled out. I would also check the ICU and provide assistance if needed, or I might help the corpsmen wash down or move equipment. We simply spent our time helping each other with whatever task needed to be completed.

Once I had ascertained that all the tasks were completed and that no one needed assistance, I would return to the porch, joining others who had gathered there. We would often read our letters from home to each other or share photos we received of our loved ones. Our conversations covered many topics, including what was going on in the world, what our lives and our stateside homes were like, and what might be in store for us in the future. We gradually began to know and understand one another well, and we formed a strong bond of friendship and developed a solid foundation of being a family.

One day we hosted a "Mexican Fiesta Happy Hour" to celebrate the birthday of one of the OR nurses, Lt. (jg) Alex Devilla. I had received a package filled with salsa, nachos, tortilla chips, and a variety of other Mexican delicacies. Others contributed goodies they had either purchased at the exchange or received in one of their own care packages sent from home. Alex's birthday cake was made from two slices of pound cake smeared with icing. The icing was made from several packages of dried cocoa mix diluted with a few drops of water. Both the pound cake and the cocoa mix had been retrieved from the contents of our MREs, and even though the cocoa-frosted birthday cake measured no more than four by six inches, we passed it around and each person was able to take a tiny piece. We sang, we laughed, and we joked around. Our spirits were indeed high.

Charlie Surgical Company personnel began showing up at Camp Chesty six days after we arrived. They were moved up from their previous position, Camp Viper, located near the oil fields of Al Bashra with expectations of moving quickly to whatever area might encounter the majority of fighting and the most casualties. They were told not to unpack or set up their hospital tents, so they erected only their berthing tents. They were to remain on standby and ready to move forward as soon as they received orders to do so.

We were happy to see the folks from Charlie Company again, and we welcomed them to Camp Chesty by hosting a special enchilada dinner. Both companies mingled and talked for hours, sharing stories of where we had been and what had happened to us. We swapped specific information on ways in which to conserve our dwindling medical and surgical supplies in preparation for future needs. We also shared information with them about Camp Chesty in hopes of easing their adjustment and adaptation to the sparse environment that had become our home.

We would continue to see our buddies from Charlie Company frequently because they would wander over to the OR porch on a daily basis trying to find something to do to pass the time, whether that meant reading hometown newspapers or outdated magazines or simply finding someone to talk with. Because they had not set up their ORs or wards and were not caring for patients, they were bored and unsettled and growing weary. Having experienced the same faltering spirits while our own company waited to move from Camp Guadalcanal, we

understood their angst, malaise, and disheartenment on a deep personal level and tried diligently to help bolster their flagging morale. We
may have been assigned to two different and distinct companies, but
we were all in the same boat, and it made little difference to us that our
"boat" was now anchored in the landlocked, barren dirt of central
Iraq, where the single water source was the water buffalo. We were all
navy shipmates and would serve as primary supports for one another
with as much diligence and determination as we could.

As Bravo Company's caseload began to diminish and fewer frontline casualties arrived who required surgical intervention, we started to
think about and plan for our futures. I spent a lot of time reflecting on
my upcoming retirement from the navy. My approved date for retiring
was 1 August 2003, and I thought about whether I really wanted a formal ceremony organized and conducted to celebrate my twenty-five
years of service. The events and experiences of being in Iraq had significantly changed my perspective, my desires, and my attitude.

Leaving the navy quietly and without formality or fanfare was an
option I was finding to be more desirable. I really had no way of knowing whether I would be back in the States when my retirement date
arrived, and as every day passed, being so far away on the other side of
the world, I could not fathom how I could possibly organize a formal,
traditional retirement ceremony. I had no means by which to communicate with those in the United States other than by writing letters, and
the postal service was extremely unreliable. Mailed items were often
not delivered for weeks or months. Many times I wondered whether
my family and friends were actually receiving the letters I sent to them.
This inability to communicate was frustrating, and I simply could not
see how I could plan a retirement ceremony while I was in the midst of
a war zone.

In addition to this issue regarding faulty and unreliable communi-
cation, I knew I would never leave the Bravo Surgical Company until
we all were able to go home together. We were a team, a family, and I
was not about to leave them even if my retirement date should occur
and I was still in Iraq. I had made that decision even before leaving
Camp Lejeune, and I was steadfast in my resolve.

Having many days of idle time with little more to do than think, I found myself consumed with these thoughts about my retirement. I believed I was meant to be in Iraq. This belief was substantiated by similarities and coincidences I had noted between the very beginning of my navy career and what were now the final days of my career. I was still wearing the dog tags around my neck that I had first been issued, and I had departed for both boot camp and Kuwait on the same day in February, albeit twenty-seven years apart. The combat troops to whom I had administered anesthesia since I had been in Iraq made me proud to be a nurse anesthetist, a navy nurse, and I was humbled by the thought that my contribution to my country was that which I was now doing in Iraq. Others had given and will continue to give so much more, and I knew the navy could give me no higher honor than what I had experienced simply by caring for the young soldiers who were being entrusted into my care.

I had previously chosen 25 July 2003 as my designated retirement ceremony date, and I knew my friends and family were making plans and arrangements to attend. I felt an urgent need to tell them about my desire not to have a retirement ceremony before they finalized their schedules and travel arrangements. I desperately wanted and needed to talk with Jeryl to try to explain my change of heart, with the hope that she would understand and be willing to inform others.

Nine days after arriving at Camp Chesty, we were given an opportunity to make a five-minute "morale phone call" to the States using the company's one and only Meridian satellite phone, which was located in the administration tent. Once again, we stood in line for our turn to use the phone, all the while praying that the person whom we were calling would pick up. I tried to calculate the best time stateside when Jeryl would be available and figured it to be around noon EST. Shortly after 7 PM Iraq time, I placed my call, and Jeryl picked up on the other end.

Hearing her voice was beyond wonderful. Although I had received several letters from her and knew things at home were going well, hearing Jeryl's voice and being able to reassure her that I was doing well were just what I needed the most. It became more than a simple morale call; talking with her gave me comfort and a sense of peace and provided me with an opportunity to tell her of my decision not to have a formal retirement ceremony. Our allotted five minutes of "phone voice time" was strictly regulated and went by quickly. We both had so much more to talk about and would have loved to continue talking for hours. Still, at least now we had the benefit of making phone calls stateside even though the opportunities were strictly monitored and infrequent.

Within two weeks after arriving at Camp Chesty, we had made it our home, a relatively comfortable, familiar, stable, and secure environment. We were working together and living together as a well-established, caring, and compassionate family. We looked out for one another, doing such things as sacrificing our own daily MRE rations to subsidize those who were losing weight.

Together we also battled the constant, unrelenting wind, which we found was affecting our health. The wind never seemed to ease up, and every day I jokingly asked "Allah" to make it stop. Allah refused to answer my prayers, and I began to believe he hated us, or perhaps me because I was Lutheran. All I really knew was that the wind continued to blow dirt and grit over everything and was a major player in contaminating our food.

As more and more of us began to experience gastrointestinal problems, we realized that in addition to the unsanitary conditions of the fly-infested bathroom stalls, the wind was indiscriminately and unmercifully delivering contaminants from the burn pit onto our food. The burn pit was a dug-out hole where everything was burned: the barrels of human waste from the bathroom stalls, everyday garbage, and the human tissue and body parts removed during surgical procedures. This burn pit was located upwind and in proximity to where we were served our meals. The wind served as conduit, very possibly sprinkling the hot meals we enjoyed with filthy contaminants and disease-causing agents.

Once we identified what was probably causing the gastrointestinal ailments affecting our battle buddies, meal service was moved, and many of us returned to sustaining ourselves full time with the MREs we were issued and personally maintained.

On 18 April 2003, Good Friday, we received good news. Instead of maintaining a full surgical support company at Camp Chesty, the Marine Corps general in authority reassessed the original plan and decided that the number of surgical cases being received did not warrant a full company made up of two hundred personnel, two ORs, and three postoperative wards. The plan was altered so that the site maintained an FRSS unit, an STP, and one ward, allowing the rest of us to move on. We were excited and looked forward to returning to Camp Coyote in Kuwait, knowing that from there we would soon be returning to the good old USA.

Each day we observed more and more marine units leaving Camp Chesty to return to Kuwait. When more than a hundred members of Charlie Company were suddenly transferred with little advance notice, we thought we would be next to go. So, we began to break down portions of our camp, disassembling OR number one and one of the wards and packing the tents and equipment into the ISO containers. Our spirits were high as we made individual preparations for moving on. We repacked our Alice packs and seabags, burned our blood-soaked MOPP gear, threw away Ziplock plastic bags containing items we could no longer identify through their dirt-covered and encrusted exteriors, and discarded other items we had salvaged or hoarded throughout the many weeks and months of our desert journey.

Believing our departure was imminent, we even used some of the distilled-water supply reserved to sterilize surgical instruments to wash our hair, which was something we had not been able to do since leaving Kuwait. Because this new plan called for us to retrograde directly to Kuwait, we believed that we would not be setting up the ORs again and that these jugs of water were going to be disposed of instead of being packed. By washing our hair, we simply thought we were putting the water to good use because the contents would not be needed in the future. We were ready to go, and as soon as we received the official word of our departure time and date, we could be completely packed, set, and ready to move on in just a few short hours.

Camp Chesty had been our home and had served us well, but we were ready to leave and were eager to return to Kuwait. Kuwait represented just one more step closer to returning to the United States. We were finally headed home, or so we thought.

# 21

# STUCK IN IRAQ

On 24 April 2003, the nineteenth day after arriving at Camp Chesty, I awoke at 5:30 AM. My seabag was packed and ready for transport, and having been previously notified that I was included on the list of one hundred scheduled to leave for Kuwait that day, I was very excited. Everything was set, and I was really looking forward to leaving Iraq.

We were all eager to attend the 6:30 AM "all hands" muster to learn the details of our transportation to Kuwait. Our sense of excitement, knowing we would soon be taking our first step toward returning to the States, was palpable, and we could not help but smile. Then the muster meeting began, and our smiles were quickly replaced by frowns, and our sense of excitement was replaced by anger, disappointment, and mumbled curses. We were informed that all movement to Kuwait was on hold. Instead of moving south, all of us would now be heading east to a place called Camp Geiger, which was located on the outskirts of Al Kut, Iraq.

The remainder of the day was spent taking down and packing up the second OR and all of the wards. Our berthing tents would stay up until after the evening meal to provide us with some form of shade in the blistering 108-degree weather. This long day, which had begun with high spirits and then turned quickly to major disappointment, moved further on to nothing more than hot, dirty, backbreaking labor. As I settled my exhausted body onto my cot at the end of the day, I looked up at the stars and wondered what the future might bring. What would our next camp be like? How long would we be there? When would we get out of Iraq and go home?

We mustered at 7:30 AM on 25 April and were told to clean up any remaining trash around the camp, a task we had performed every time prior to leaving an area. It was an extremely windy day, one where wearing our goggles was a necessity and performing any simple task required tremendous strength and effort. The wind was so strong and relentless that for every four steps we took forward, it would push us two steps back. Fortunately, all our gear had been packed and loaded into the ISO containers the previous day, and once the area had been cleared of trash, we had little more to do than wait for the transport trucks to arrive.

Grouped into transport stix, we huddled together, attempting to protect one another from the progressively strengthening wind. Without tents to shield us, dirt and sand caked our clothing and goggles, and the wait time seemed interminable. At 9:30 AM the truck convoy arrived. Wearing our Alice packs, helmets, flak jackets, and goggles, and carrying our pistols, we boarded the open-bed seven-ton trucks, where we would continue to sit for an additional ninety minutes waiting for the ISO containers to be loaded. Because the truck beds were not covered or shielded by canopies, we continued to be totally exposed to the relentless swirling wind and dirt of the Iraqi desert.

The route the convoy would take to Camp Geiger would entail passing through two Iraqi villages. Once again we were cautioned not to give those who might approach the trucks anything or to take anything from them. We were also not to hesitate in firing our pistols if we believed our lives to be in danger.

The thirty-mile trip east to Camp Geiger took four long hours, including the ninety-minute waiting period prior to departing. This trip was not anything like the convoy travel we survived when we had moved from Camp Hasty to Camp Anderson or from Camp Anderson to Camp Chesty. Despite being openly exposed on the back of the trucks, we heard no sounds of gunfire or deadly blasts from mortars. Our only enemies were the blazing sun and relentless wind blowing dirt into our noses and our mouths and covering everything.

As we passed through the two Iraqi villages, men, women, and children ran up to the trucks waving, giving "thumbs-up" signs, blowing kisses, and shouting, "Thank you!" and "We love you!" Their gestures were very moving, and I was thankful I had my goggles on so no one would witness my tears. The everyday common citizens of Iraq seemed to genuinely appreciate our efforts to liberate their country and to provide them with a sense of freedom unlike anything they had ever experienced or could have possibly dreamed of before.

Camp Geiger was located slightly south of Al Kut and had been secured by the marines several days prior to our arrival. This extensive base appeared to have once served as an Iraqi airport facility and contained several aircraft airstrips or runways. Some of the runways were intact, whereas others were totally bomb-ridden, resembling nothing more than a trash pile of huge, broken concrete slabs. Bombshells, casings, and exploded vehicles were strewn throughout the area. Numerous old pyramid-shaped hangars made of concrete were situated throughout this concertina wire–encased compound where several marine and other military units were based. The FRSS, STP, and ward we had sent in advance were all housed in one of the intact hangars.

Our first task on arrival was to off-load some of our own ill and debilitated hospital company staff from the convoy ambulances and into the hangar ward that had been set up earlier by the FRSS and STP personnel. At least twenty-five members of our company continued to experience significant gastrointestinal symptoms that required intravenous fluid hydration therapy to replace vital body fluids lost from constant, severe diarrhea and vomiting. Because the FRSS was set up and immediately available to perform any surgeries that might be needed, we were not required to establish our ORs immediately. Still, we were quick to identify various spaces within this hangar where we would station the Bravo Surgical Company's two ORs, laboratory, pharmacy, ICU, and administrative support office.

Despite the fierce wind, we were able to erect a few tents to provide us with some shelter during the night. Whereas some chose to find a place to sleep in the hangar, and others simply found a place on the exposed ground where they would lie down and throw a tarp over themselves, I opted to find berthing in one of the tents.

Weary from fighting the wind all day long, being jostled about in the beds of the convoy trucks, and assisting with the transfer of our ill comrades into the ward, we looked forward to retiring for the night with hopes of having a quiet, restful night's sleep. At 10:30, just as we were beginning to retire to our sleeping bags, we heard shouts to "turn out all lights!" These shouts were immediately followed by the clatter and rat-a-tat-tat of automatic weapons being fired. We had no idea where the gunfire was coming from, who was firing at whom, or even whether we were the targets of the gunfire. Having no bunkers in which to take cover, we could do little more than lie in our sleeping bags, watch the flashes created by the constant firing, and listen to the loud noise created by the gunshots. Fortunately, the skirmish lasted only thirty minutes. We would hear the next morning that the shooting was between Iraqi and Iraqi and that our American troops were not involved.

Attempting to sleep that first night at Camp Geiger, even after the unsettling firefight had been resolved, was not easy. Our bodies were covered with dirt, and our noses were so full of grit and grime that it was hard to breathe. Our sleeping bags were filthier than ever before, which was something I thought would have been impossible after our experiences at Camp Guadalcanal, Camp Anderson, and Camp Chesty. The wind continued its relentless assault on us, and around 1 AM rain and lightning began. I believed I had moved even further into hell and found this place the most depressing of the four camps we had now been in.

The next morning we surveyed the damage caused by the torrential rain and strong wind we had endured during the predawn storm and found mud and dirt caked everywhere. One of our newly erected tents had also been destroyed. We mustered for a head count, and though we had all survived the night unscathed, several more members of our company were beginning to exhibit the dreaded, miserable symptoms of gastroenteritis. After tending to those who were ill, those of us who continued to be reasonably healthy started unloading the ISO containers to set up the ORs. We were scheduled to open for business the next morning, which would allow the FRSS crew, who had been providing surgical care to the wounded in that area prior to our arrival, to break down, pack up, and move on to another location.

We began setting up the ORs in two small enclosed rooms located within the interior of the hangar. A third adjacent room would be used to store supplies but could be easily converted into an additional OR on demand. The rooms smelled musky and dank, and they were dirty, with mold deeply embedded in the concrete walls. Guided by the expertise of the OR nurse, Cdr. Joel Parker, we thoroughly scrubbed every inch of the walls and floor with a strong chemical solution before we brought in the first piece of equipment. We were fortunate to have such a cleaning fanatic as Commander Parker among our ranks, and although the rooms were not sterile, they were as clean as they could possibly be.

The hangar was supplied with electricity, so we strung wires and lightbulbs on the ceiling of these rooms. In addition, we knew we would need to use our individual headlamps (lights attached to our heads with hook-and-loop strapping) in order to have adequate illumination for performing surgical procedures. The small size of the rooms limited us to one table, one anesthesia machine, and one anesthesia vaporizer per room, so we could not set up two OR tables head-to-head in each. In the third room we prepared tables, supplies, and anesthesia equipment for easy assemblage in case we quickly needed an additional OR suite.

Working within such a small, dark, airless space would be challenging. Simply bringing the patient into the doorway and placing that person on the table would require significant jiggling and jostling that would cause the wounded individual additional pain and suffering. There was scarce room in which to maneuver, and we would miss the head-to-head OR table setup that allowed the two anesthesia providers to assist one another. Cleaning the floor of blood and body fluids would also be a challenge. This floor was solid, so we could no longer simply shovel the fluids out as we had done on the dirt floors in our ORs at Camp Anderson and Camp Chesty.

The rear portion of the hangar was lined with approximately twenty to fifty cots set up in rows. This area, farthest from the hangar opening, would serve as the general medical-surgical ward because it was warmer, providing some protection from the cold nighttime temperatures. Empty AMMAL containers, which were large, durable containers in which we packed medical supplies, were stacked up to mark off a smaller area that could serve as an ICU. Initially we placed our ill personnel in every other cot in this ward to prevent cross contamination, but we soon began placing them side by side as more and more fell ill with each passing day. I had often read about the devastating impact gastrointestinal illness had on the troops during wartime and was now witnessing it firsthand.

Those suffering with severe diarrhea and vomiting were totally incapacitated. They were too weak to walk and even required assistance just to stand. They found it impossible to go to the designated bathroom area located outside the hangar, so we erected a small indoor structure consisting of a bucket covered by a plank of wood with a hole in it. This small john facility provided some semblance of privacy but little else. I felt so fortunate that I remained healthy and uninfected.

After preparing the ORs so they were ready to take in any wounded who might require surgery, we turned our attention toward establishing our company's berthing tents and ancillary structures.

Once these structures were in place, we had an opportunity to explore the Camp Geiger compound further.

Located near us was a secure detention holding facility for EPWs. Consisting of a pit approximately six feet deep, this facility was surrounded by additional concertina wire. Ten to fifteen Iraqi prisoners resided there under the constant watch of heavily armed marine guards. The prisoners were prevented from talking with one another or communicating through motions or gestures, but I never witnessed any mistreatment of those prisoners by the marines.

A marine support unit had converted one of the compound's structures into a chow hall. It was located within easy walking distance of the Bravo Surgical Company's designated encampment, and we would go to this facility for our morning and evening meals. After entering the food tent and standing in line while we received our allotted scoops of heated MRE foods on a paper tray and plate, we would exit that tent and go into another to eat. This dining tent featured tables built from plywood and molded plastic chairs with backs. It was wonderful to sit in a chair and actually be able to sit back in it!

Personnel at the chow hall were responsible for providing meals to several units stationed at Camp Geiger, and the flow of troops and other military personnel in and out of this facility was constant. As much as we might have wanted to sit and socialize, the chow hall was for eating only, not a place to spend time idly talking about the events of the day. Others were constantly arriving and needed a place to sit and eat. "Get your food, eat it as quickly as possible, and move on" was the order of the day.

A shower facility was constructed and was available for use by both males and females at separate and specified times, one hour in the morning and one hour in the evening per gender. This tent facility had a concrete floor, and on entering it we would disrobe and place our clothes, towels, and other belongings on one of the benches or tables provided before going into the large eight-showerhead bathing tent through the connected back flap of the changing area. The warm water spraying from the shower fixtures was fantastic, and, for a moment, I would know what it was like to feel clean again. The shower was a luxury compared to trying to wash the dirt and grime from my body using a water-filled Tupperware bowl and an old rag. Unfortunately, the clean feeling we all obtained from the shower would be short lived. Because the shower facility was a significant distance from our company's camp area, by the time we walked back—our wet hair and damp skin being pounded by the wind-blown desert dirt—we would once again be sporting a dirty brown coating all over our bodies. We were beginning to understand how a powdered doughnut must feel.

Farther down the road from our company's location, a marine unit had set up a thirty-two-inch television, with about five chairs facing it, in one of the hangars. The television was turned on twenty-four hours a day, and we were able to access CNN News and the Fox News Channel. I began to go over to that hangar every evening at 6:30 to watch an hour-long broadcast of world events. Ever since my nine weeks at boot camp, I had despised being in situations where I had no way of being informed about world events. Getting news from those who were in my immediate world was highly unreliable and uninformative. What we knew was either rumor or gossip based on very few actual facts. On that one television, which was cherished by many in our camp, I was able to watch broadcasts about military actions that indicated this Iraqi war was coming to an end and that we would soon be heading home.

Another hangar not too far from us was home to what we called the "community center." It featured about fifty chairs, set up theater style, and we were welcome to come in any night at eight o'clock to watch a movie projected onto the hangar's concrete wall.

We also had available to us a post office and small exchange. Mail was catching up to us, and once again we began receiving packages from home filled with wonderful and very welcome treats. Because we were now receiving these kinds of packages, the junk food available at our small exchange, located in a tent with a maximum occupancy of ten people, was not in high demand. Still, we would frequently take the thirty-minute walk to the exchange if we just wanted to see whether anything new had arrived or if we needed something to do.

Seven bathroom facilities, what we referred to as "poopers," were constructed. They were located in the immediate vicinity of our company's designated camp area. Each pooper featured three wooden sides, a canvas flap front door, a hard wooden seat with a hole cut out, and a drum that had been cut in half placed underneath the cutaway seat to collect our waste. The duty crew would take turns burning this waste material along with whatever trash and other debris our camp produced. One of the best things about Camp Geiger was the waste/trash–burning process. Unlike the situation at Camp Chesty, the burning of trash and waste took place far away from our chow hall, allowing for minimal contamination of our food.

After spending nine days at Camp Geiger, exploring its few but very positive features, establishing a routine, and even beginning to meet and know some of our marine unit neighbors, I realized it was not as depressing a place as I had initially thought. This camp provided a few more niceties and accoutrements than what had been available at Camp Chesty. Most of all, we were finally in a place with reasonably clean air.

We received no casualties of combat during our days at Camp Geiger. The majority of our patient-care activities involved caring for those suffering from severe gastrointestinal illnesses, many of whom were our own company members. A few surgeries would be performed in our ORs, but they would be relatively minor cases, and most would involve work-related medical problems or injuries sustained in motor vehicle accidents.

Feeling relatively safe and knowing that Camp Geiger was heavily guarded and protected by the marines, I was able to resume my daily routine of running despite having little tread remaining on the soles of my running shoes. I was regularly joined by Commander Sheppard and Lt. Steve Wingfield, the dentist assigned to Bravo Company, and we would run an average of twelve miles a day.

I was keeping my body fit and healthy. I ate as well as I possibly could with the MRE food provided, maintained my physical activity on a regular basis, and rested. I also took specific and determined steps to stay as clean as possible, including washing my hands frequently and diligently with an antiseptic solution. To this day I do not know whether these personal health measures were what actually prevented me from contracting the draining, debilitating, and miserable gastrointestinal problems and symptoms suffered by so many others. All I know is that, for whatever reason, I was one of the more fortunate, and my general good health remained intact.

On 30 April 2003 (1 May 2003 in the United States), several of us went to the television hangar to watch President George W. Bush announce that the mission of Operation Iraqi Freedom had been officially accomplished. Hearing this news, we were eager to move on, to go back to our homes in the States. We even began wondering about the possibility of being able to go home by way of Baghdad. We had spent more than three months in Kuwait and Iraq, where we performed our duties as best we could under primitive, rudimentary conditions, and had survived the sand, dirt, flies, relentless wind, scorching daytime heat, freezing nights, and constant threat of being killed. President Bush's words "mission accomplished" meant to us that the coalition forces had successfully liberated Baghdad and that it was safe. Why could we not just travel there, hop on a plane at Baghdad International Airport, and fly back to the United States?

None of us wanted to stay in Iraq any longer than was needed, and we certainly did not want to relocate to yet another camp within the Iraqi border. We also did not want to return to Camp Guadalcanal in Kuwait. Having "been there, done that," we believed we knew what it would be like to return to that dug-out sand pit. It would be like going back to the beginning. Hearing that Kuwait was overloaded with troops and military personnel returning stateside, we had no desire to trade our good life for another bottleneck that would consist of hurry up and wait, and wait, and wait some more for the next available transport. As rustic as the conditions at Camp Geiger were, we were settled, we had developed a relatively comfortable and secure routine, and we had made it our home. The only other home we wanted to travel to was our personal one in the United States.

As is more often true than not when one is a member of the military, and especially when that military of which you are a member is located in a foreign, war-torn country, you quickly realize that your personal desires will never match the reality that lies before you. Despite our personal desires to go home as expeditiously as possible, we would be forced to encounter one more very meaningful and memorable venture before finally returning to the States.

# 22

# BACK TO THE BEGINNING

On 7 May 2003, we were told that on 10 May, 125 of us would be leaving Camp Geiger to return to Kuwait. Instead of that desired flight from Baghdad to our homes in the United States, we were indeed going to return to the beginning. As disappointing as that news was, we consoled ourselves with the thought that at least we would be taking one more step closer to returning home.

We began packing up our gear, breaking down the two ORs, and dismantling some of our berthing tents. The departure plan called for the first group to leave on 10 May; those left behind were to hold fast until the FRSS and STP arrived. Once those groups were set up and prepared to care for patients, the remaining members of Bravo Surgical Company would be transported to Kuwait.

Having moved out of my assigned berthing tent to allow those remaining behind to move into it, I slept under the stars the night of 9 May. Awakening at 4:45 the following morning, I completed packing my Alice pack with essential supplies that were to sustain us for possibly five to seven days; dressed in full gear including helmet, flak vest, and pistol; and reported for muster at 6:30. At 7 AM the seven-ton trucks arrived and began the round-robin process of transporting us to the runway tarmac where we would await the arrival of the C-130s that would fly us to Kuwait. We were told we had what was termed "priority status," so we anticipated only a short wait on the tarmac before being allowed to board the planes.

I had been assigned to transportation stix number three and arrived at the tarmac at 7:30 AM. In addition to our own company's personnel arriving for transportation, several hundred troops from marine units also arrived and began the process of waiting to board flights to Kuwait. As the C-130s landed, we grew excited, expecting to be the first group to be boarded. Our excitement quickly turned to bitter disappointment when we were told to hold fast and wait. Instead of being boarded onto the planes, we sat on the concrete part of the tarmac with little shade in 110-degree heat and watched as one group of marines after another boarded the C-130s and flew away. Each time a plane would land, our hopes of boarding would rise, only to be repeatedly squelched. Hour after hour passed; we waited and waited. Because we were in a "priority status," we were required to remain grouped in our transport stix and allowed to leave the area only briefly to relieve ourselves in one of the fly-infested, wooden four-seater (no individual privacy stalls) "restroom facilities" or behind a bush. Our meager sustenance came in the form of MREs and water that was brought to refill our canteens.

At 7 PM, after waiting on the tarmac for close to twelve long, miserable hours, we were informed that no more planes would be arriving and that we needed to find a spot on the concrete to sleep. I pulled out my sleeping bag and bedded down for the night underneath the stars. At 9:45 PM, less than two hours later, I was awakened by shouts and yelling that directed transport stix numbers one through three to get up, pack up their gear, and within ten minutes be prepared to board a C-130 that had unexpectedly arrived. After what I had endured over the previous fourteen hours, this order to hurry up and pack was the last straw, and despite being assigned to stix number three, I did not move. I believed nothing at this point and doubted that the C-130 was truly going to board our company's personnel and fly to Kuwait that night.

I was also tired of being ordered around by senior enlisted personnel who had no real positional authority and were often misinformed. We all had the same information, and history had shown that that information was, more often than not, unreliable and sometimes totally invalid. Having been bullied and pushed around by senior enlisted during the early days of my career, and now being an exhausted commander on the verge of retirement who had just survived many brutal and harrowing days of war, I was finished with being jerked around. I just wanted to go back to sleep. I woke up long enough to say "Go to hell" to the chief petty officer yelling at me, and to tell my running buddies that I wished them a safe trip and I would see them in Kuwait. Then I simply rolled over in my sleeping bag and went back to sleep, thinking, "What's one more day?" and believing that tomorrow would be better. Lt. Cdr. Necia Williams would also stay behind, and she became my new battle buddy.

On Sunday, 11 May (Mother's Day), I awoke at 5 AM still lying on the concrete tarmac underneath the wide-open skies of Iraq. I watched as a wild dog wandered around the area in search of whatever scrap of food it could find. Responding to the call of nature, I got up from my sleeping area and wandered to a nearby bush to relieve myself. Fortunately, the wild dog was not aggressive toward me and seemed to be only a little curious.

Approximately sixty Bravo Surgical Company personnel remained on the tarmac, and as we began the process of packing up our gear, we all wondered how long we would wait for a flight or whether there would even be a plane that would take us to Kuwait that day. It seemed ironic that our travel back to the beginning would be so similar to our transport experience leaving Kuwait and flying to Iraq—get up, hurry up, wait for transportation, wait some more, and then wait even longer. We all hoped the similarity between that experience and the one we were currently enduring would end with the dawning of this new day.

Once our gear was packed and we again attired ourselves in full gear, including carrying our Alice packs on our backs, we began the process of waiting once again. This time, however, we were the only personnel at the airstrip, so our chances of actually boarding a flight looked hopeful. Our hopes were temporarily dashed when C-130s began to land but, instead of taking us on board, started loading up outgoing cargo. Finally, shortly after noon, another C-130 landed, and we actually began to board the plane. Because I had given up my stix position the previous night, I was "punished" for this uncooperative behavior by being placed in the last stix group to board. Frankly, I did not give a damn. We were all going to be boarding the plane, and it mattered little to me that I would be the very last one on.

Thirty hours after arriving at the runway tarmac, we clambered up the plane's rear loading ramp and found a place to settle within the plane's cavernous and sparsely furnished interior. The day was brutally hot; the temperature exceeded 120 degrees. This heat, compounded by the heat of the plane's engines and the fact that we were all attired in full gear, made us all sweat profusely. Still, the plane was not as crowded as the one on which we had flown into Iraq on 2 April, forty long, torturous days earlier, nor did we zigzag our way through the sky to avoid being targets of ground-to-air missiles. No one vomited on him- or herself or onto a nearby buddy, and within forty-five minutes we landed in Kuwait on a sand airstrip immediately outside the perimeter of Camp Okinawa (one of many small camps within our original larger encampment called Camp Coyote). We had finally returned to the beginning. And even though we did not desire this delay in our progress toward returning to our real homes in the United States, what we found there—what we would experience and discover about ourselves—ultimately made our transition stateside the best it could possibly have been.

# 23

# WELCOME TO
# THE "HOLIDAY INN"

W hen we landed in Kuwait, the seven-ton trucks were there on the man-made airstrip waiting to transport us to our new temporary home at Camp Okinawa. Not having to endure yet another transport delay surprised us, and we almost did not know how to cope as we were smoothly transported to our new location. Various refinements and enhancements had been made to Camp Okinawa while we had been in Iraq, and it was definitely not the same place we had previously visited. Alpha Surgical Company, who had remained there throughout the official combat days of Operation Iraqi Freedom, might not have appreciated the rather rustic and rudimentary luxuries offered at Camp Okinawa on a daily basis, but we members of Bravo Surgical Company thought we had arrived at the Holiday Inn!

Upon arriving at Camp Okinawa, we were nicely and even politely told to line up and place our gear in a designated area. Instead of being yelled at or harshly ordered to do this or to do that, we were being talked to in a kind, respectful, and civil manner. After receiving a warm welcome by those greeting us and managing our arrival, we were invited to go to the chow hall tent where we could consume as much soda and ice cream as the human system could tolerate. We were also told that soda and ice cream would be available twenty-four hours a day and that we need not hesitate to come back for more. Being treated with such respect and kindness was almost overwhelming.

Instead of wanting to go to the chow hall to partake in the delectable treats being offered, though, what I desired most was to find Cdr. Vanessa Noggle, a family nurse practitioner and friend I had known for eighteen years. Vanessa and I had developed a true bond of friendship over those many years that could not be broken or shaken despite the many miles that often separated us when we were assigned to various duty stations throughout the States and overseas. We stayed close through frequent phone calls, letters, and visits with one another, spending hours sharing the stories of our lives and simply being there for each other during the good times and the bad. I had received a letter from her weeks earlier telling me that she had been assigned to a reservist surgical company that had deployed to Kuwait. I hoped to find her among the ranks of Fox Company, now based somewhere within the compound of Camp Okinawa, to hug her and be hugged in return.

Despite my eagerness to find Vanessa, I went with the group to the chow hall and enjoyed a delicious cold Coke, something I had not tasted in several long weeks. I was in awe as I looked around. The chow hall had a clean wooden floor, numerous tables adorned with plastic decorated tablecloths, and chairs with backs. We even had the option of sitting at a table in a real chair outside the mess tent if we so desired! The sodas and other refreshments were ice cold and were stored in a real temperature-controlled cooler. Food, real food vice MRE food, was prepared on grills. In the center of the messing facility was a buffet table where different cereals, fruits, drinks, and other nourishment would be set out and available for the taking at various mealtimes. The sight of all this luxury was mind-boggling.

After thoroughly enjoying our sodas and ice cream treats, we returned to gather our gear and then were graciously and politely escorted to our berthing tents. Some of my battle buddies in Bravo Surgical Company who had departed for Kuwait on the first plane had made special arrangements for my sleeping area to be near the door of the tent. I was deeply touched by their thoughtful and considerate gesture.

Our berthing tents had a wooden floor and electricity, and although no cots were available to us, we really did not care. Lying on the wooden floors was a lot cleaner than lying directly on the ground, and the overall conditions were much more pleasant than what we had had for forty harrowing days amidst the sparse, hostile, coarse land of Iraq. Eventually, even air-conditioning would be installed in our berthing tents and would be greatly appreciated as the outside temperature began to soar well above 100 degrees every day.

Still very eager to find Vanessa, I quickly dropped my Alice pack and other miscellaneous gear on the floor of my new berthing space and asked whether anyone knew where I might be able to find Fox Company. I was told they lived on the other side of the berm, but this made no sense to me until I began walking around the camp's compound.

Camp Okinawa had significantly expanded during the days we were in Iraq. Now serving as the home of approximately twelve thousand personnel attached to various surgical support companies (Alpha, Bravo, Charlie, Echo, and Fox), it was like a little city carved out of the sand in the middle of the Kuwaiti desert. One of the sand berm walls that had originally enclosed the camp now ran through the middle of it, for the camp had doubled in size. An opening in this sand wall allowed access to the other side, and I found that walking through this opening was similar to leaving one city and entering another.

As I made my way through the berm's opening, I saw tents and people everywhere; everyone seemed to be involved in one of a wide array of activities. Some were moving in and out of tents on their own personal missions, walking toward some specific destination. Others were sitting, relaxing, reading, or engaged in conversation. Still others were running, playing volleyball, or participating with their friends in some other outdoor sport or recreational activity. It was an unbelievable sight, and it represented such normalcy, something I had not experienced or witnessed in a very long time. Although we had tried to re-create a relatively "normal" American way of life at the various camps while in Iraq, what I had just entered into was the real thing. Everyone was relaxed, unafraid, and, most striking of all, free to be and to do whatever they desired.

Wandering through this "mini city," I would stop at various tents and ask, "Where's the female officers' tent?" Even when I was given directions, I was still not sure I knew where I was going because all the tents looked alike, with the exception of one tent that displayed an inflatable swimming pool in the "front yard" that someone had brought from the States. The sight of that swimming pool sitting ridiculously, yet so proudly, before one of the berthing tents made me laugh. It was such an unexpected sight, so cute and so very American. I thought, "This is really great! This is Club Med!"

Rounding one corner after another, all the while asking the location of the female officers' tent, I began to feel frustrated. Then, as I turned one final corner, I noticed a tent that had erected a web-netting roof to serve as cover for an outside patio area. Several people were sitting there in chairs, and I caught a glimpse of Vanessa getting up from her chair and starting to enter the tent. While her back was to me, I said, "Hey, girl." When she turned around and saw me, her expression was one of confusion, followed by shocked recognition, and then warm, loving smiles. I immediately started crying, and as we hugged one another I felt the comfort, love, and all-encompassing sense of safety of being home. That day, Mother's Day of 2003, was the happiest day I had experienced since first arriving in Kuwait on 17 February.

Vanessa, whom I fondly call "Ness," would later tell me, "When I looked at you, all I thought was that you looked like death." I had lost a lot of weight, my eyes were sunken, my clothes were filthy, I was filthy, and my sand-filled hair was in total disarray. While Ness was hugging me on that special and memorable day in Kuwait, she said, "Come on. We're getting out of here," and she immediately guided me away from those gathered on the patio. Not until later would I realize that one of those sitting there was Lt. Cdr. Mike DiBonaventura, who had been stationed with me as an ensign twelve long years earlier on board the USNS *Mercy*. The navy was indeed a very small world.

After Ness and I walked, talked, laughed, and savored this incredible and very special time of togetherness, I went to clean up. We soon met again at the mess tent. As we moved through the line to get our food, the food server asked, "Commander, what would you like? A hamburger or a hot dog?" It was a hard choice for me because I truly wanted to eat everything. When I responded, "May I have both?" I was told that I had to make one choice. I ultimately chose the hamburger. As soon as we sat down to eat, Ness immediately took the hot dog off her plate and placed it on mine. As I tried to object to this kindness, she stopped me and said, "Cheryl, just eat it." And so I would, along with my own hamburger, baked beans, potato chips, ketchup, mustard, and just about anything else in sight. I would experience some painful gastrointestinal issues later in the evening, but that food—the first real food I had eaten in six weeks—tasted so good going down.

The three weeks I spent at Camp Okinawa were important and meaningful ones. Life was good, and every day I would discover and enjoy many wonderful amenities available at this compound. I had been deprived of so many simple, yet meaningful, aspects of normal living; the days spent at Camp Okinawa gave me an opportunity to rediscover them—gradually, and with a greatly renewed appreciation. While I had been in Iraq, I had thought many times of several friends' pets whose lives were much better than mine, but now those days of deprivation were truly over.

This "Holiday Inn" in the middle of the Kuwaiti desert, in addition to having the luxurious wooden floors on which to sleep and real food that could be consumed in a warm, friendly, and laid-back atmosphere, also had shower facilities that were in enclosed solid-sided trailers. The water that sprayed from the shower nozzles was warm and plentiful, and the shower stalls were private and clean. Our access to these shower facilities may have been restricted to taking one shower every other day, but gradually we began to feel clean again.

Our days of locating a bush, digging a hole in the desert dirt, or visiting a fly-infested and crudely erected wooden pooper in order to relieve ourselves or to change tampons were also over. Scattered throughout the compound were multiple modular, commercially constructed, plastic-sided molded portajohns that provided privacy and comfort. These "restrooms" truly did provide an opportunity to rest versus swatting at flies or trying to ensure that the canvas flap door did not fly open or into your face. I was so excited about the portajohns that I found myself describing them twice in the same letter to my sister.

One of the tents had been converted into a small workout gymnasium that contained free weights, a rowing machine, a stationary bike, and a treadmill, all donated to the camp by the fleet hospital from Portsmouth, which had also been briefly detailed here. Also included in this tent, in an area separated by a line on the floor, were a television, several small card tables, and chairs. This section was set up as a place to sit back, relax, watch television, or do whatever leisure activity we desired. The only regulation associated with this free-time recreational area was that we had to be in uniform. Also, we were not allowed to cross that designated line on the floor if we were in gym clothes.

It was from the television located in this recreation area that I learned the fate of Jeff, the young marine I had helped at Camp Anderson. Although I was not a direct witness to it, Dave Sheppard informed me that while he was watching a news broadcast, he recognized Jeff as this very special patient of mine. The broadcast showed Jeff at the National Naval Medical Center in Bethesda, Maryland, being presented a Purple Heart by President Bush. It was such a wonderful ending to that story; I could not have been more delighted, knowing that Jeff had made it home to the States safe and alive.

Shortly after we arrived, our mail was delivered. I received close to thirty care packages, many postmarked mid-February. Our mail had obviously been held while we were in Iraq, which was unfortunate because we could have benefited greatly from the many wonderful personal care items and savory treats we were now receiving but did not necessarily need. Opening all of those packages was wonderfully exciting, even better than opening gifts on Christmas morning. My thoughtful and generous friends and family had really been thinking of me and had sent a lot of great stuff.

Others in the Bravo Surgical Company were also beginning to receive their mail, and one day a total of seventy-six boxes were delivered to our berthing tent. Because we knew we would be limited in what we could take back home with us, we set up a mini "Sam's Club" and invited all of our buddies to come over and "shop." It was actually much better than any such store stateside, for all our merchandise was free for the taking. After those desiring to do so had rummaged through the contents of this store, we carefully packaged many of the remaining items and sent them north into Iraq for use by the sailors and marines left behind.

Our mission while at Camp Okinawa was simple. We were to decompress, await the arrival of our equipment from Camp Geiger, either discard or clean that equipment for repackaging into the ISO containers, and simply wait our turn to fly home to the United States. After discovering all the luxuries and the fun to be had with my buddies at Camp Okinawa, I did not care whether we would be leaving in two days or two weeks. I was doing fine physically, and I felt much more human and in great spirits. So were the rest of my colleagues who had been in Iraq. It was easy to identify those from Bravo Surgical Company; we were the ones who considered the camp to be a Holiday Inn and had absolutely no complaints.

The numerous berthing tents, chow halls, administration, postal services, and recreational centers of Camp Okinawa were nicely laid out. We had plenty of room in between the tents to erect makeshift outdoor patios or to develop a "yard of sand"—or even to display an inflatable pool. We also had a large perimeter area where we could walk or run. Once again, I began a daily regimen of walking and running and would often be joined by my former battle buddies Dave Sheppard and Steve Wingfield. Even though I would need to get up at 4:30 AM in order to avoid the tremendously hot and stifling heat of the day, it was great to be running or power walking again. These activities added just another element to my sense of feeling normal again.

Physically, I was doing well, with the exception of experiencing some achy muscles and joint pain. Considering that I was forty-five years old, I did not think I was doing too badly. I had pretty much kept up with the younger troops as we had crawled in and out of the backs of all those seven-ton trucks. Still, the aches and pains I experienced reminded me of my "older age status" on a daily basis. On days when the intensity of these maladies increased, I would modify my physical activity to working out on the gym equipment or walking instead of running. Each day I could feel myself getting stronger.

Once our gear arrived from Iraq, the enlisted members of our company worked diligently to clean and repack it into ISO containers for shipment back to the United States. These young men and women, who refused to let the officers assist, would work at night in order to avoid the stifling heat of the day that averaged close to 120 degrees. We watched out for them, providing them with special treats, goodies, and refreshments, and ensuring that the process was conducted in a relaxed, nondemanding, and civil manner.

We knew our time for going home was drawing near when we were instructed to complete the post-deployment medical screening process. The process required the completion of several forms, including a variety of questions specific to our physical and mental health. After individually answering the questions and submitting these completed questionnaires to the screeners, we discovered that all of us had indicated "yes" to the question, "Was there ever a time you felt like you were going to be killed?" For many, the times we believed that we might be killed had occurred during the convoy rides we had taken

from Camp Hasty to Camp Anderson and then farther north to Camp
Chesty. Having had several days to relax and reflect on our time in
Iraq, we were becoming more and more aware of just how much peril
our lives had actually been in.

Some reservists assigned to Camp Okinawa had brought their own
cell phones to Kuwait, and we were allowed to use them to call our
families stateside. We would sign up on a list to reserve a time to use
whoever's phone was chosen and would pay $1.00 or more per minute
to make the call. After we had been informed that we would be leaving
and going back to our real homes in the States, I used one of these
phones to call Jeryl. It was 26 May, Memorial Day, and I said to her,
"The next time you hear from me, I will have my foot on American
soil." Having already contacted the navy's Plans, Operations and Medical Intelligence (POMI) office, Jeryl seemed to know more about my
homecoming than I did and was already making arrangements for herself, her husband, Jim, and my mom to meet me when I arrived at
Portsmouth. I so much wanted to be with them, to hug them, and to
express my love for them. I had missed them deeply while on this journey, and now that we had a definite date scheduled for our return, I
found it hard to wait to get home and be with my family.

The three weeks spent at Camp Okinawa allowed me to regain a sense
of normalcy physically, mentally, and emotionally. Being surrounded
and comforted by very dear friends and buddies, I began to feel safe,
secure, and confident. I learned to relax, to find fun and humor in the
smallest things, and simply to enjoy life again. I was now much cleaner,
healthier, stronger, and much better groomed than when I had first
arrived.

I had also successfully discarded some very unattractive habits and
traits that may have been useful in times of deprivation but would be
viewed as rude and unrefined in civilized society. I had once jokingly
written to my sister, "I apologize ahead when I come to visit you if I

use the same paper towel to wipe my face, blow my nose, then head to your restroom taking the paper towel with me." Because this had been something we would do so often while in Iraq, it had become a habit, and had I not had the opportunity at Camp Okinawa for this gradual reentry into a civil society, I might have actually done just that.

# 24

# THERE'S NO PLACE LIKE HOME

For several weeks we had been anticipating a departure date from Kuwait sometime between 1 and 7 June. Although we were more comfortable at Camp Okinawa than anywhere else we had been since leaving the States, we were nonetheless very excited and thoroughly delighted when informed we would be flying out and heading home on 30 May.

Our final days at Camp Okinawa were spent discarding items we definitely did not want to bring back into our homes in the States. We trashed filthy clothing, old shoes, worn-out dingy socks, Ziplock bags filled with old coffee packets or other items we had scrounged off the ground or out of dumpsters, leftover MRE foods, and worn plastic containers. Everything we saved and planned to take back to the States had to be carefully inspected for "war trophies." War trophies were items that would be considered in poor taste, such as guns, knives, explosives, bullets, or other items that might have been taken from an EPW or from the ground in Iraq. Prior to the official inspection of our belongings, "amnesty barrels" had been placed at designated areas throughout the camp. Any individuals who might have these trophies in their possession could drop the items off in the barrels, and no questions would be asked.

The inspection process was thorough. All of us reported to a specified inspection area where we would dump the contents of our seabags and Alice packs onto a tarp. Then the inspectors would carefully examine every article of clothing, every bottle and container, and any other item we had. Bomb-sniffing dogs were also used to ensure that none of us had any explosive materials. Once the belongings were inspected and cleared, we repacked the bags, and then they were sealed with a special tamperproof lock before being securely stored in ISO containers for transport to the States. The only thing we would be allowed to carry on board our transport vehicles would be one small carry-on bag, the contents of which would also be thoroughly inspected before we boarded the plane.

Vanessa and I met for breakfast that morning, and saying good-bye to one another was painful and sad. She had been such a tremendous support for me by providing guidance, a sense of safety, a listening ear, and even a shoulder to cry on. I had hoped she would be leaving with us, and I would miss not seeing her on a daily basis. Still, despite her having to remain a few more days before coming home, I knew our sense of solidarity and unconditional friendship would always remain intact. Saying good-bye to her that day was the hardest moment I had experienced in weeks.

Once again we were formed into transport stix, and then we waited for buses to arrive to take us to the airport. Unlike the uncomfortable old school buses in which we were first transported into the Camp Coyote complex on 17 February, these buses were large commercial tour buses, and our ride to Kuwaiti International Airport was comfortable, enjoyable, and filled with a pervasive sense of excitement.

Arriving at the airport, we disembarked the buses and were escorted to one of several tents. On entering, we presented our identification cards and progressed to a closed-off area at the rear of the ID verification station. Several tables were stationed in this area, and we stopped here to present our carry-on bags for the inspection of contents. Even the contents of our uniform pockets were thoroughly searched and carefully scrutinized. Once officially cleared, we were guided into yet another tent, where we were instructed to remain until our plane was ready to board.

The plane that would fly us home was a large United Airlines carrier that proudly displayed the American flag on its side. As we made our way into the plane's plush interior, I stopped at the top of the steps leading to the plane's doorway, turned, and looked around, and it hit me deep within my heart—we were finally going home after having survived so much! It was such a powerful feeling, one too overwhelming and soul wrenching to be described in mere words.

Just like the plane that had carried us to Kuwait, this aircraft was decorated with American flags displayed everywhere. The flight attendants also proudly wore uniforms of red, white, and blue, and they eagerly welcomed us on board with genuine smiles and warm hospitality. We could hear in their voices, see in their faces, and observe in their gracious and kind actions toward us that they were proud of us and of what we had done while in the service of our country. If their actions and the words written in numerous letters we had received were true, we knew we were returning home to a nation proud of our military sailors, soldiers, marines, and air force and one that was most grateful for the many sacrifices we had made to help make our country a safer place to live.

On the flight to Germany we spent our time sleeping, talking, and eating. I had found that whenever I was offered food, I would eat it even when I was not really hungry. Remembering well those many days of subsisting on nothing more than MRE rations and not always sure when I would be able to eat again, when food was put in front of me, I ate it all.

Following a brief refueling stop in Germany, we were once again in the air heading home. With each passing hour that moved us closer to the United States, our excitement grew, and so did the volume of our conversations. We did not talk of the past, for our minds and hearts were now directed strictly toward the future. We talked about what we were going to do first when we stepped back on American soil, what we had missed the most, and how much we hoped and prayed our loved ones would be there to welcome us home. Our heightened emotions were almost palpable, and we could barely wait for the plane to land at Cherry Point, North Carolina.

Family and friends of those from Camp Lejeune and Portsmouth were discouraged from coming to the airstrip to meet us. Cherry Point was simply to serve as a place for us to disembark the plane, load ourselves with our belongings onto buses, and be transported expeditiously to Camp Lejeune. As soon as the plane's landing gear touched the runway tarmac, we all cheered. The sound was deafening. We were all so thrilled to be home, back on American soil again, and we knew we would shortly be reunited with our loved ones.

During the bus ride to Camp Lejeune, I sat at the window and found myself in awe as I looked out at all the greenery, the flowers, the gas stations, the grocery stores, and so much more that I had once taken for granted. Most touching and appreciated of all were the general signs, such as "We love you troops" and "Welcome home troops," and the individual personalized signs displaying greetings, support, and love for a special friend or family member serving in the armed forces. Signs, banners, and flags were displayed everywhere: in yards, hanging from trees, draped across doors, and hanging from windows. Whether the signs were made specifically for a friend or family member serving in Iraq or ones placed by everyday Americans unattached to the military, it mattered not. Those signs, the flags, that simple show of support, appreciation, respect, and gratitude were an incredible sight to see, and they moved me deeply.

Arriving at the armory at Camp Lejeune, we turned in our weapons. I was fortunate enough to be one of the first to move through this process; more than two hundred of us were trying to complete this same task. I then went in search of a phone. I had promised Jeryl that the next time she heard from me I would be on American soil, and now that I was, I could not wait to call her.

I found my way into some administrative offices located at the back of the armory where a lieutenant (junior grade) stood. He approached me respectfully and compassionately, and while placing his arm around me, he said, "Welcome home, Commander. What can I do for you today?" "I would really just like to call my family," I responded. Pointing at the nearest phone, he said, "There's the phone, Commander. Call anybody that you want."

I called Jeryl's number, and I was thrilled when she picked up on the other end. Hearing my voice, she immediately started crying and said, "You're on American soil!" I told her that I was at Camp Lejeune and that we were expected to leave for Portsmouth, Virginia, around 5 PM. She told me that she, Jim, and my mother would be leaving Pennsylvania shortly and would be in Virginia around nine o'clock that evening.

From the armory, the reloaded buses moved toward the staging field where families and friends waited. Even from a distance we could see that a massive crowd had gathered. Some carried signs, and others had balloons, flowers, or some other meaningful token of love and welcome. Those with family members waiting in the crowd quickly scrambled off the buses, and the air was filled with excited and joyful exclamations as hugs and kisses were exchanged between husbands, wives, children, and friends. It was a beautiful, touching, and very moving sight to behold. Those of us who did not have family waiting at Camp Lejeune busied ourselves with unloading the seabags and gear from the buses.

Around five o'clock in the afternoon, those needing transportation to Portsmouth climbed aboard a Bluebird school bus for the final four-hour trip north. Despite the smallness of the bus seats, this bus was not as crowded as when we first traveled to Camp Lejeune because several families and friends of our Portsmouth comrades had met them at Camp Lejeune and were transporting them home in their own vehicles. Each of us riding in the bus had an entire seat to ourselves, and the trip was comfortable because we were not wedged in like sardines, as had been the case before.

Arriving at the NMC Portsmouth compound, we were off-loaded from the bus at the base gym. More families were eagerly waiting to be reunited with their loved ones, and the deeply moving scene of warm hugs and joyful kisses being exchanged repeated itself once more. Unfortunately, my family was not there, so after catching a ride to the hospital, I called my friend Cdr. Tam Martin. Tam had continually stayed in close contact with Jeryl, and having been notified I was expected to arrive sometime that afternoon, she was somewhere in the hospital waiting for me. On receiving my call, she immediately came to meet me at the hospital's information desk. Our reunion was a very emotional one. Tam had been there to bid me farewell when I deployed 29 January and was now there for me again, welcoming me back home after 122 days spent on a journey unlike any I had ever experienced before.

Tam and I exchanged hugs and shed tears of joy, and then we quickly threw my seabags into the car and left the base. On the way to my house we made a quick stop at a local grocery store and bought some ice-cold Corona beers. It was dark when we arrived at my house, but I could see it was completely intact and awaiting my return. Walking into the gate of my own backyard was an incredibly surreal experience. Was I really home? Was this a dream?

As I went up onto the deck in my backyard, I immediately removed my boots, boots that I had worn throughout my journey and that I swore I would never wear again or even bring into my house. Tam graciously handed me an open beer, and I began walking barefoot around my yard. I stopped and looked at every single flower, touching them, smelling them, and loving and cherishing each of them. Yes, I was really home; no dream could possibly be this good.

Because it was 9:30 at night, I am sure that if anyone had observed Tam and I laughing and hugging and looking at and touching all the flowers while we wandered around the yard barefoot with beer in hand, they would have immediately thought we were both crazy or very much under the influence. Personally, I did feel under the influence, the influence of absolute joy, true happiness, and pure delight at finally being home.

While we were still out wandering around the yard, I heard the sound of car doors closing. My back gate, through which we had entered, was still open. I turned around, and walking through the gate were my mom, Jim, and Jeryl. My heart exploded with joy. I grabbed my mom and squeezed her tight. She was crying, I was crying, we all were crying. I remember little of what we said on seeing one another, but I will never forget how loved I felt being hugged by my sister and my mother, and having the arms of Jim encircle me in a big bear hug, welcoming me home.

Jeryl was disappointed that I had arrived at my house before they did. She had bought numerous small American flags and had wanted desperately to have them placed all throughout the yard and garden so that I would see them on my arrival. I am not sure when she actually did place those flags, but maybe it was sometime in the middle of the night. What I do know is that when I awoke the next morning, my yard and garden were filled with flowers and flags. It was an incredible sight and such a heartfelt symbol of how proud she was and how much she loved me.

I found it hard to believe I was really home and surrounded by my family. At times, I felt as though I had entered into an alternate reality as I wandered around looking at everything, talking, laughing, and simply cherishing the sense of safety and security that can only be achieved in one's own home. I had spent so many months adjusting to various living conditions, making sandpits as homey as possible, holding ropes and pounding stakes to prevent the wind from destroying our tent houses, and never feeling quite safe. Being home, in my own real home, made me realize there really is no place like home—it was safe and it was secure, and as a result of our small contribution toward the war on terror, I hoped it would remain so for many years to come.

# EPILOGUE

Although I arrived home sixty days prior to my official retirement date, I would never again enter the operating theater of a military facility as an active-duty anesthesia provider. Having enough days to start terminal leave prior to retiring, I chose instead to end my career by providing anesthesia in a tent in Iraq to a seriously wounded soldier. I could ask for no higher honor bestowed on me than this, my tribute to the navy and to my country.

I chose not to have a formal retirement ceremony. Instead, I celebrated the end of my twenty-five years of naval service with a gathering at my home, surrounded by my family, friends, and flowers, all of which I had longed to see for months.

The past year has been one of transition: retiring from an organization after twenty-five years of service, returning from a war, and adjusting to a civilian lifestyle. I am reminded on a daily basis of the war that continues and the young lives that will be either horribly changed or lost as a result of it. At times, I cannot help but relive the painful experiences I witnessed in the final months of my military career, but I have also been able to pull from those memories positive lessons learned.

Perhaps the greatest lesson I learned is the question of evaluating one's own vulnerability to one's own death. For eight years, my cousin Kathy lived each day as though it was her last. She desperately tried to teach her family the meaning of this. I cannot say I truly understood her teaching until I went to Iraq. My life was changed, and now I understand what Kathy meant.

I continue to practice my love of anesthesia at a local surgery center. Not a day goes by without my thinking about the tremendous training I received from and the commitment instilled in me by the Navy Nurse Corps to provide care to our active-duty frontline sailors and marines. Despite how hectic my civilian job may get at times, it has become easy for me to put life back into perspective simply by reminding myself, silently, "At least no one took a shot at me today."

# Support Our Troops

Today thousands of active duty military personnel continue to protect the United States of America, bravely serving our nation in hotbeds of violence like Iraq and Afghanistan.

The Department of Defense–sponsored Web site *America Supports You—Our Military Men and Women* (http://www.americasupportsyou. mil/) lists many independent organizations that are ready and willing to help you support the troops. These organizations will help you send morale-boosting mail, messages, and packages to the troops. Through these organizations you may also donate frequent flyer miles, fund scholarships for military children, give gift certificates and phone cards, and provide help for the wounded and homes for disabled troops.

Some of the organizations included on the Web site are

The Injured Marine Semper Fi Fund
825 College Blvd Suite 102
PMB 609
Oceanside, CA 92057
Web site: http://www.semperfifund.org/

AdoptaPlatoon Soldier Support Effort
AdoptaPlatoon-Nanny Fran
P.O. Box 1457
Seabrook, NH 03874
Web site: http://adoptaplatoon.org

Letters From Home Program
c/o Chris and Jim Jovenitti
6631 Ridgway Jbg. Road
Johnsonburg, PA 15845
Web site: http://lettersfromhomeprogram.org

# About the Authors

**Cdr. Cheryl L. Ruff,** U.S. Navy Nurse Corps (Ret.), presently lives in Portsmouth, Virginia, and is a nurse anesthetist at the Chesapeake Surgery Center. She enjoys traveling, running, gardening, and spending time with family, friends, and her beloved cocker spaniel, Misty.

**Cdr. K. Sue Roper** is a twenty-one-year veteran of the U.S. Navy Nurse Corps. While on active duty she served at various duty stations within the continental United States and overseas, specializing in the fields of psychiatric nursing and education management. Following her retirement from the navy in 1995, she was appointed to the adjunct faculty of Old Dominion University, Norfolk, Virginia.

Author of numerous published magazine articles detailing current events, special interests, and personality profiles, she is the editor-in-chief of the *NNCA News,* the official newsmagazine of the Navy Nurse Corps Association.

Commander Roper lives in Virginia Beach, Virginia, and enjoys traveling the country in her RV, collecting and recording the stories of those she meets and documenting the vast and illustrious history of those who have served or are presently serving in the U.S. Navy Nurse Corps.